Jane McNabb

Esther

Royal Rescue

7-Session Bible Study

Esther: Royal Rescue
A Good Book Guide

This edition printed 2025.

Published by The Good Book Company

thegoodbook.com | thegoodbook.co.uk
thegoodbook.com.au | thegoodbook.co.nz

A CIP catalogue record for this book is available from the British Library.

Design by André Parker and Drew McCall

ISBN: 9781802541649 | JOB-008397 | Printed in India

Contents

Introduction

One of the Bible writers described God's word as "a lamp for my feet, a light on my path" (Psalm 119:105, NIV). God gave us the Bible to tell us about who he is and what he wants for us. He speaks through it by his Spirit and lights our way through life.

That means that we need to look carefully at the Bible and uncover its meaning—but we also need to apply what we've discovered to our lives.

Good Book Guides are designed to help you do just that. The sessions in this book are interactive and easy to lead. They're perfect for use in groups or for personal study.

Let's take a look at what is included in each session.

Talkabout: Every session starts with an ice-breaker question, designed to get people talking around a subject that links to the Bible study.

Investigate: These questions help you explore what the passage is about.

Apply: These questions are designed to get you thinking practically: what does this Bible teaching mean for you and your church?

Explore More: These optional sections help you to go deeper or to explore another part of the Bible which connects with the main passage.

Getting Personal: These sections are a chance for personal reflection. Some groups may feel comfortable discussing these, but you may prefer to look at them quietly as individuals instead—or leave them out.

Pray: Here, you're invited to pray in the light of the truths and challenges you've seen in the study.

Each session is also designed to be easily split into two! Watch out for the **Apply** section that comes halfway through, and stop there if you haven't got time to do the whole thing in one go.

In the back of the book, you'll find a **Leader's Guide**, which provides helpful notes on every question, along with everything else that group leaders need in order to facilitate a great session and help the group uncover the riches of God's light-giving word.

Why Study Esther?

As a Christian, do you believe that God is always with you? Are you certain that he is always working things out for your good? Have you got full assurance that he loves you and cares for you as nobody else in the whole world does?

When things are going well in our lives, we are more likely to say yes to these questions. When things are bleak… when the future looks ominous… when we're struggling with our sin and the consequences of our sin… well, that's when the rubber hits the road. Those are the times when we're likely to ask, *Does God truly love me? Is he really in control? Does he actually know what he is doing? Will he rescue me from this?*

These are exactly the kinds of questions which the book of Esther poses. God's chosen and special people are facing a crisis of epic proportions. Not only are they exiled far from their home in the land of Judah but they are threatened with persecution on an unprecedented scale. Their whole future hangs in the balance.

Thankfully, there is someone working behind the scenes—one who is in charge, who loves his people passionately and who will always rescue them. Strangely, this deliverer is not mentioned by name. Yet so convincing is his presence that when the drama ends there is only one question to ask: Who else, other than God, could have done this?

This same God offers tremendous hope to us all. The whole of humanity has been in rebellion and exile from him, and now his eternal judgment lies ahead of us. We too face a crisis of epic proportions. We too desperately need rescuing.

Incredibly our Judge has become our Deliverer. The task that God gave Esther of saving the Jews is a preview of the greatest rescue mission of all—God sending Christ to save all his people, everywhere and throughout history. And Christians today also have a part in God's great mission as God sends us to the ends of the earth to spread the good news about Jesus. And so the story of Esther, and how God used her to deliver his people from their enemies, is a story for our time too.

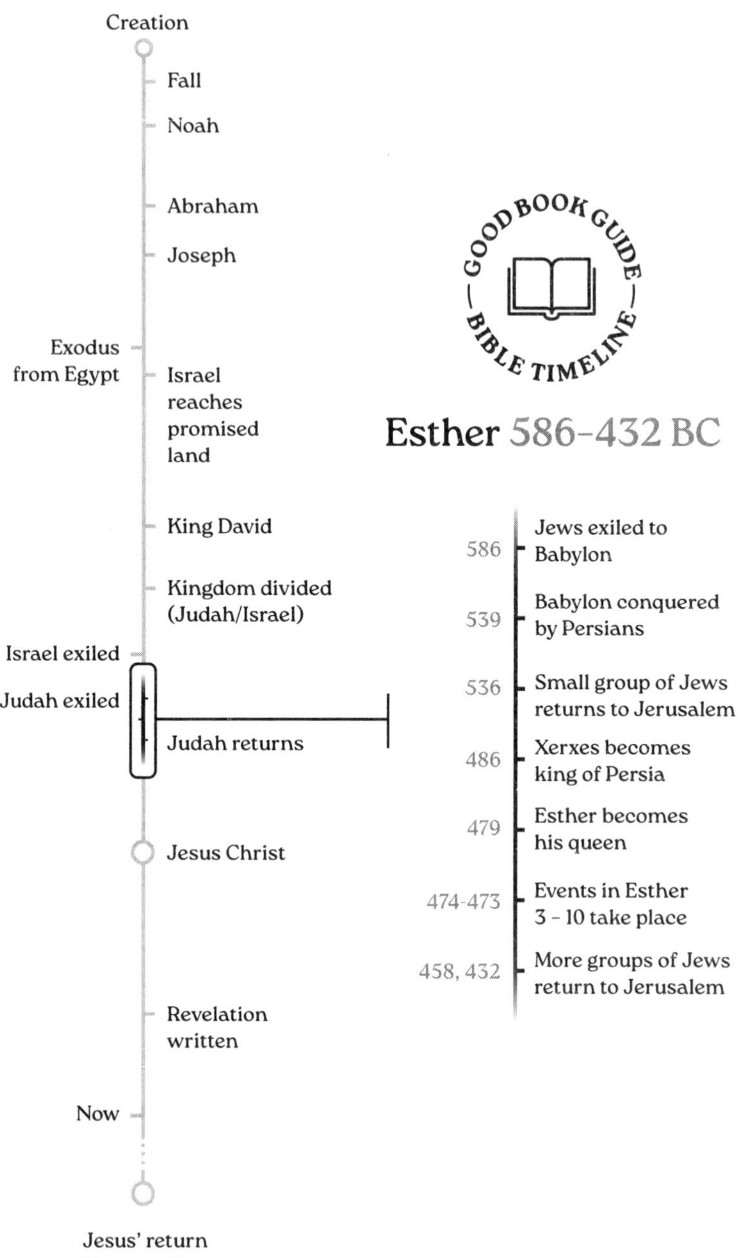

Creation
Fall
Noah
Abraham
Joseph
Exodus from Egypt
Israel reaches promised land
King David
Kingdom divided (Judah/Israel)
Israel exiled
Judah exiled
Judah returns
Jesus Christ
Revelation written
Now
Jesus' return
New creation
GOOD BOOK GUIDE
BIBLE TIMELINE
Esther 586-432 BC
586 Jews exiled to Babylon
539 Babylon conquered by Persians
536 Small group of Jews returns to Jerusalem
486 Xerxes becomes king of Persia
479 Esther becomes his queen
474-473 Events in Esther 3 - 10 take place
458, 432 More groups of Jews return to Jerusalem

1

Party Time at the Palace

Esther 1

The Story So Far...

The story of Esther takes place in the time of the Jewish exile under Persian rule. The exile happened because the Jews rebelled against God—despite God frequently warning them to turn back to him. In 586 BC Judah, which was all that remained of the ancient nation of Israel, was invaded by the Babylonians, and the people either killed or taken into exile.

But about 50 years later, Babylon was conquered by the Medo-Persians. The Medo-Persian Empire was the largest the world had seen. Cyrus the Great was the founder of the Medo-Persian Empire; and Xerxes, the king of Persia who features in the book of Esther, was the grandson of Cyrus.

By the time of Esther, some Jews had already returned to Judah, though most were scattered throughout the Medo-Persian Empire.

Talkabout

1. What words would you use to describe 21st-century culture?

Investigate

📖 **Read Esther 1:1-9**

DICTIONARY

Cush (v 1): land south of Egypt.
Susa (v 2): a Persian city (in modern-day Iran).
Porphyry (v 6): a type of rock.

2. What do we learn here about the Persian ruler, King Xerxes, and his empire?

3. Three celebrations are mentioned. What was the purpose of each?
   - Party 1 (v 3-4)
   - Party 2 (v 5-8)
   - Party 3 (v 9)

4. Xerxes seems very proud of his rule and his kingdom. By contrast, what was the attitude of Israel's greatest ruler, King David? Read 1 Chronicles 29:10-13.

- The Jewish prophet Isaiah lived before the Babylonian conquest and Jewish exile. What did Isaiah specifically prophesy about Cyrus (founder of the Persian Empire) in Isaiah 45:1-7, 12-13?

5. Imagine yourselves in the shoes of God's people, the Jews, living in exile in Persia at this time. How do you think they might feel?

- What would make it difficult for them to remain the distinctive people of God, do you think?

Apply

6. Read Philippians 3:20 and 1 Peter 2:11. In what sense are true Christians living in exile?

- How is the experience of being a Christian in our world similar to the experience of the Jews living in the Persian Empire of King Xerxes?

- What makes it difficult for us to be the distinctive people of God?

Getting Personal | OPTIONAL

As a Christian, have you realised that you are in exile in this world?

Do you sometimes fear that God is not in control? Or that the world's wealth and power are greater than God's?

How should the truth about God's sovereignty (1 Chronicles 29:10-13) both encourage and humble you?

Investigate

Read Esther 1:10-22

DICTIONARY

Eunuchs (v 10): castrated men, who often worked as palace officials.

Edict (v 20): an official order from the king.

7. What more do we learn about Xerxes here?

8. Who does he blame for the crisis that follows his wife's refusal to comply with his command? (See verse 15.)

- Do you think he was justified in deposing the queen? Who or what else could be responsible for this humiliating situation?

9. What was the ripple effect of this incident, both personally and nationally?

Explore More | OPTIONAL

The New Testament apostles describe the world outside of Christ—the culture and behaviour of the Roman Empire. It's strikingly similar to the Persian culture of Esther's day, and to Western secular society as well.

Read Ephesians 2:1-3; Philippians 3:18-19; Colossians 3:5-10; 1 Peter 4:1-4

- What are the behaviour and cultures of the world like, according to the New Testament apostles?
- What drives them to be like this?
- Is this how we see our society?
- How will God's people (true Christians) stand out?

Apply

10. There are many similarities between Persian culture and our own culture today. Briefly identify some of the specific problems that we, our families and our churches face, living as God's people in a secular culture.

- Read 1 Corinthians 6:9-11. What hope does the gospel bring?

11. In this session we have seen the consequences of Xerxes' drunkenness: pride and showing off; petulant, uncontrolled anger; and blame-shifting. When Christians fall into sinful behaviours like these, how does it affect those around us?

- Read James 4:6-10. What do we need to do when we fall into these kinds of sins?

Getting Personal | OPTIONAL

Where do you most feel the pressure to act like the non-Christian world around you? Think of one specific way in which you need to repent and change this week.

Pray

As a group:

- *Praise God for his sovereignty over all the kingdoms of this world, and his continued faithfulness to his promises.*
- *Thank God for the hope that we have in the gospel, and for Christ, who came to restore what sin has broken.*

On your own:

- *Spend time repenting of any specific sin in your own life that has been highlighted in this study.*

2

Waiting in the Wings

Esther 2

The Story So Far...

God's people are in exile in Persia, where people live in rebellion against God, and the king has rejected his queen. But God remains sovereign and faithful to his promises.

Talkabout

1. Describe a time and situation when you felt extremely uncomfortable and out of place. How did it turn out?

Investigate

Read Esther 2

DICTIONARY

Harem (v 3): part of a palace reserved for women, including royal wives.
Myrrh (v 12): a strong-smelling substance used for perfume or skin care.

Concubines (v 14): women who slept with a king, but weren't legally married to him—a sort of live-in lover.

At least three years have passed since Vashti was deposed. (See 1:3; 2:12; 2:16.) There has been no queen since then, and around this time Xerxes also suffers a shocking and devastating defeat against the Greeks (the Battle of Salamis in the sixth year of his reign).

2. What is so appealing to Xerxes about the advice of the royal attendants, do you think?

- How does this fit with what we learned about him in session 1?

3. Read Proverbs 31:10-11, 30. Compare the qualities that were thought to be most desirable in a new queen with those that are most valued by God.

Apply

4. In which ways does our society share "Persian values" when it comes to physical appearance? What problems can this create for us (whether we're male or female)?

- Read 1 Samuel 16:7. How are Christians to be different on this issue of physical appearance?

- Read 1 Peter 3:3-4. How can we help each other to live by God's values?

Getting Personal | OPTIONAL

Honestly examine your own perception of beauty. To what extent do you share Persian (i.e. worldly) values, and how does this play out in your life?

What can you do practically to value beauty in the way God does?

Investigate

5. Look at the introductions in Esther 2:5-7. What do we learn about these two new characters?
   - Mordecai
   - Esther

6. Describe the experiences that Esther went through in verses 8-18. Would it have been an exciting adventure or a terrifying ordeal? Why do you think that?

- Why do you think Mordecai forbade Esther to reveal her nationality and family background (v 10)?

7. Read Genesis 39:2-5, 20-23. Although God is not mentioned, how can we see that he is with Esther?

8. How does Proverbs 21:1 relate to Esther 2:17?

Explore More | OPTIONAL

God used Xerxes' vanity and selfishness to place one of his people, Esther, at the centre of Persian power in preparation for a great rescue of his people. This is a pattern seen throughout Scripture. Look at the following Bible events and discuss how each reveals God's complete sovereignty over evil.

Read Genesis 50:18-20

- How did God use the hatred of Joseph's brothers towards Joseph for the benefit of his people?

Read Exodus 5:1-8, 19-22; 6:1-7

- How did God use the furious refusal of Pharaoh to obey his word for the benefit of his people?

Read Acts 2:22-24

- How did God use the hatred of the Jewish leaders towards Jesus to benefit his people?

- What can we learn from these true stories that will help us in times when evil seems to be winning over good?

Apply

9. Esther was separated from her family and people. Give examples of periods of isolation and change that we sometimes face. When might we feel isolated because we are Christians?

    - Why do you think Christians often struggle in their faith at these times? On the other hand, how can these experiences be a blessing?

    - Read John 10:29 and Romans 8:31-33, 38-39. What assurances do these verses give us, no matter what we're experiencing?

10. Is it possible to prepare ourselves in advance for such challenges? How?

Investigate

11. What evidence is there in this chapter that Mordecai is a man of integrity, love and wisdom?

12. Read 1 Peter 3:3-4. How does Esther show the true inner beauty that God values?

Getting Personal | OPTIONAL

How would you have coped in Esther's or Mordecai's place?

What has challenged you most as you've looked at their lives in this chapter?

How can you be like them in the situation that you are in?

Pray

As a group:

- *Praise God that he never abandons us, even in the most difficult circumstances.*
- *Pray for those experiencing isolating or bewildering circumstances, basing your prayers on what you have learned this session.*

On your own:

- *Ask God to help you put into practice the things you have been challenged by in the lives of Esther and Mordecai.*

3

The Gathering Storm

Esther 3

The Story So Far...

God's people are in exile in Persia, where people live in rebellion against God. But God remains sovereign and faithful to his promises.

A Jewish woman, Esther, has been selected to be King Xerxes' new queen. Esther's experience shows that God is keeping his promise to be with his people.

Talkabout

1. Who do you think are the opponents of God's people today? How do they show their opposition?

Investigate

📖 **Read Esther 3:1-6**

DICTIONARY

Agagite (v 1): an Amalekite from the tribe of Agag. Centuries before, Israel defeated and executed King Agag (1 Samuel 15:32-33). The then king of Israel, Saul, was part of Mordecai's tribe (Benjamin).

In verses 1-2 we meet Haman the Agagite, an up-and-coming Persian noble, who will play a major part in the story. After generations of hostility between the Agagites and the Jews (see dictionary), Haman's appointment as prime minister is bad news for Mordecai.

2. In chapter 3:10 Haman is called "the enemy of the Jews". Look at verses 1-6. What are the first signs of this?

    - How could this enmity help to explain 2:10 and 20?

3. In verses 1-5, what are the signs that Mordecai is a man of principle and courage?

    - What drives Mordecai's behaviour, do you think? And what has no effect on his behaviour?

    - How do we know that he isn't a rebel against the king? (See 2:21-22.)

Apply

4. Read Ephesians 6:10-13. What more does this tell us about the enemies of God's people today?

- What two strategies do God's enemies use against his people? (See verses 11 and 13. Hint: think about what the "day of evil" is.)

5. Why do we often find it difficult to take a stand and remain firm?

- Why is it important to do so?

Getting Personal | OPTIONAL

In what area of your life are you under attack from God's enemy? How are you doing with standing firm? What will encourage you in this?

Investigate

Read Esther 3:6-15

DICTIONARY

Cast the pur (v 7): a traditional way of making decisions, based on Persian superstition.

Ten thousand talents (v 9): about 375 tonnes (345 metric tons). That's a lot!
Satrap (v 12): local ruler.

6. How does Haman put his plan into action?

- How does he reflect the devil's strategies (Ephesians 6:11 and 13)?

7. If Haman's plot had succeeded, how would the rest of Bible history have been affected? What would the eternal consequences have been, both for Jews and non-Jews?

8. List the character traits of Haman throughout this chapter.

    - What motivates his actions?

9. You would expect the *Jews* to be devastated, but verse 15 says that the city of Susa *as a whole* was bewildered. Why might this be the case, do you think? (Jeremiah 29:4-7 might help you here.)

    - What does this show us about the hostility of people like Haman towards God and his people?

Explore More | OPTIONAL

Revelation 12 is a key passage for understanding the state of war between God and Satan. This real spiritual conflict is what fuels the people and powers of this world (like Haman) to oppose and persecute God's people (like Mordecai and the Jews in Esther's day).

Revelation 12 uses lots of symbolism:

The woman (v 1) = God's chosen people, Israel. (See Genesis 37:9.)

The dragon (v 3) = God's enemy, Satan (v 9).

The male child (v 4-5) = Jesus Christ, the King and Rescuer promised by God. (See Revelation 19:11-16, especially v 15.)

Verse 5 is shorthand for the whole of Jesus' time in our world from his birth (v 5a) to his ascension (v 5b), including his death and resurrection.

Read Revelation 12:1-10

- What was the devil's goal in verse 4? Was he successful?
- After Jesus' death, resurrection and ascension (v 5), what happened in heaven (v 7-10)?
- What has changed for Satan as a result of this (v 8, 10b)?
- What does this passage reveal about Satan's activity in Esther's time?

Apply

Sometimes we feel bewildered when we face opposition for living as followers of Jesus and telling others about him.

10. How do these verses help us to understand why this happens?
    - John 15:18-25
    - 1 Peter 4:3-4

11. How can we be encouraged when we face opposition? (Read 2 Corinthians 2:14-16.)

12. How could you now help a friend who is thinking of giving up the Christian faith because of opposition from friends and family?

Getting Personal | OPTIONAL

"If you suffer for doing good and you endure it, this is commendable before God. To this you were called, because Christ suffered for you, leaving you an example, that you should follow in his steps." (1 Peter 2:20-21)

Do you understand that this is how life as a Christian will be? How ready are you to live like this?

Pray

Let your prayers be shaped by what you have learned about...

- *Jesus' perseverance in suffering and the sacrifice he made for us.*
- *the Christian privilege of sharing in Christ's suffering.*
- *God's final and certain victory over all his enemies.*
- *the need for yourselves and for suffering Christians to stand firm.*

4

A Challenge Set

Esther 4

The Story So Far...

God's people are in exile in Persia. One of them, Esther, has become the new queen. But they now face total destruction through the scheming of the king's favourite, Haman, an enemy of God and his people.

Haman is just one agent of God's enemy, Satan, and Haman's plot against the Jews is one example of Satan's attempts to destroy God's people and God's promised Messiah. But through Christ's death on the cross, Satan and his plans have already been defeated.

Talkabout

1. Think of a time when someone personally challenged you to do something that you were afraid of. Did they convince you to do it? How?

Investigate

📖 **Read Esther 4**

DICTIONARY

Sackcloth and ashes (v 1): a way of showing mourning, distress or repentance.

Gold sceptre (v 11): a rod held by a king to show his authority, which he held out towards someone he wanted to show favour to.

2. Look at the Jews' reaction to the royal edict in verse 3. How would you describe their feelings?

3. To what extent do you think this crisis is Mordecai's fault?

4. How does Mordecai react? What does he do and where does he go (v 1-8)?

    - How can we tell that despite his distress Mordecai still trusts in God (v 14)?

5. Esther seems afraid in verse 11. Why, do you think? (It may help to look up Esther 1:12, 19; 2:20; 3:4, 11; 4:2; and also Nehemiah 2:2.)

6. When Mordecai challenges Esther in verses 13 and 14, what arguments does he use?

   - Do you think this was an easy plea to make? Why / why not?

7. Read Jeremiah 29:10-14. How do Mordecai's words in verse 14 line up with this message from God through the prophet Jeremiah?

8. What do Mordecai's words in verses 13-14 tell us about…
   - God?

   - Mordecai's own faith?

- Mordecai's relationship with Esther?

Apply

9. What does verse 14b suggest about the relationship between God's sovereignty and our responsibility? (See also Jeremiah 1:4-7.)

10. Read Ephesians 2:8-10. How does the answer to question 9 relate to our salvation?

    - Read 2 Timothy 3:16-17. How does God equip all Christians today for "good works"?

    - So, what are the "good works" that have been prepared in advance for us to do (Ephesians 2:10)?

Explore More | OPTIONAL

In session 3's Explore More, we looked at Revelation 12:1-10. We saw that the devil's goal was to destroy God's Messiah, Jesus, but he was unsuccessful (v 4-5). There was a war in heaven (v 7), in which Satan was defeated and thrown out (v 9, 10b).

📖 **Read Revelation 12:9-12, 17**

- What was the devil doing in heaven, which he can no longer do (v 10)?
- Where is the devil now and what is he doing (v 12, 17)?
- How do God's people (Christians) now continue to fight against him (v 11)?
- What is life in this world now like for God's people (v 17; see also verse 11b)?
- Overall, is this passage encouraging or discouraging? Why?

Investigate

11. How is Esther different in verses 15-17 from the Esther of verse 11? What do you think has changed her?

Apply

12. How should we respond in a situation where we are fearful of doing what God wants? What will help us overcome our fear?

Getting Personal | OPTIONAL

Meditate on Mordecai's words in verse 14: "And who knows but that you have come to your royal position for such a time as this?"

Is there anything specific that God has been challenging you to do recently that you are fearful of?

What have you learned that will help you to obey?

How will you make sure you benefit from God's word, which equips you thoroughly for every good work?

Pray

As a group:

- *List promises that God has made to his people.*
- *Thank him for his faithfulness to each one—most of all for his promise kept of a Saviour.*
- *Pray for each other to be strengthened in faith in him.*

On your own:

- *Talk to God about the good works he has prepared for you to do.*
- *Ask him to thoroughly equip you through his word for every one of those good works.*

5

The Pride Before the Fall

Esther 4:15 - 5:14

The Story So Far...

God's people, exiled in Persia, face total destruction through the scheming of powerful Haman, an enemy of God and his people. But God has placed Esther in the position of queen, so that she can speak to the king and seek protection for her people.

Esther and her cousin, Mordecai, face great danger in resisting Haman's evil plans, but their faith in God enables them to overcome fear. Similarly, as God's people today trust in his sovereignty and faithfulness, we can be courageous witnesses of Jesus Christ in a hostile world.

Talkabout

1. Describe a time when you felt supported by the prayers and love of others.

Investigate

Read Esther 4:15-17

Although Esther has already faced some daunting experiences, she now faces the greatest challenge of her life.

2. What does Esther call the Jews in Susa to do? Why? (Read Daniel 9:3 and Joel 2:12-13.)

Apply

It's important to check that the way we pray for one another is shaped by the examples of godly and effective prayer that we find in the Bible.

3. If you had been one of the Jews asked by Esther to fast, what do you think you would have prayed for?

4. Read 2 Thessalonians 1:11-12. How and what do Paul, Silas and Timothy pray for their fellow Christians?

   - In 2 Thessalonians 3:1-2, what things do they ask their fellow Christians to pray for them?

Getting Personal | OPTIONAL

How do your prayers compare with those of Paul and his friends?

How does your commitment to prayer compare with the kind of commitment Esther requested from the Jews?

Are there any changes in your view of prayer, or your practice of prayer, that you need to make this week?

How will you make sure you benefit from God's word, which equips you thoroughly for every good work?

Investigate

📖 **Read Esther 5:1-8**

DICTIONARY

Petition (v 6): request.

5. In what ways is this an encouraging start to Esther's mission?

Xerxes seems aware that something is on Esther's mind, asking her twice what it is that she wants (verses 3 and 6).

6. Why do you think she delays making her true request on both occasions?

7. What qualities do you think she shows here?

🕮 Read Esther 5:9-14

DICTIONARY

Elevated (v 11): promoted.

8. Track Haman's changing emotions and the reasons for each one.

Haman is in a position of great power, yet emotionally he is all over the place. Esther is in a position of great weakness and vulnerability, yet she shows great patience and self-control.

9. What explains the difference between Haman's emotional instability and Esther's patience and self-control, do you think? (You might like to read Galatians 5:16-22.)

Getting Personal | OPTIONAL

Do you, like Haman, experience huge mood swings? Do anger, frustration, bitterness, anxiety, etc. regularly rob you of peace and joy? What is it that causes you to lose control? How do mood swings affect your relationships with others? Have you made the link between your mood changes and your pride, between your lack of self-control and your lack of humble dependence on God?

Apply

10. How do we change from being like Haman (an emotional rollercoaster) to being more like Esther in her patience and self-control? What guidance do these passages give us?
    - Galatians 5:19-26
    - James 4:7-10

Explore More | OPTIONAL

Read Proverbs 11:2; 29:23; 16:18

- What warnings are we given about pride?
- Why do you think God hates sinful pride?
- What does Jesus say about humility? Read Matthew 18:1-4 and Luke 18:9-14.
- How did Jesus show humility? Read 1 Peter 2:21-24.
- What does humility look like today?

Pray

As a group:

- *Thank God for the privilege of prayer.*
- *With 1 Thessalonians 1:11-12 in mind, pray for one another.*

On your own:

- *Talk to God about areas in your life where you've been challenged about your need to rely humbly on him.*

6

A Rollercoaster Ride

Esther 6 - 7

The Story So Far...

God's people, exiled in Persia, face total destruction through the scheming of Haman, an enemy of God and his people. But the new queen, Esther—a Jew—is uniquely able to speak to the king on behalf of her people. Esther and her cousin, Mordecai, find courage through their faith in God to resist Haman.

Their reliance on God is seen as Esther makes prayer a priority before action, resulting in wisdom, courage and hope which bring glory to God. Similarly, Christians bring glory to Christ as they humbly and prayerfully rely on him.

Talkabout

1. Have you ever faced something difficult, and then discovered (perhaps much later) that God was clearly working everything out behind the scenes? What was it?

Investigate

📖 **Read Esther 6**

DICTIONARY

Chronicles (v 1): historical records.
Exposed (v 2): discovered and made public.
Head covered (v 12): a sign of great distress.

We left Haman in the last session erecting a 75-foot pole/gallows on which to impale/hang Mordecai. As the news of this spreads, the Jews might well fear that God has not heard them. Time for their deliverance seems to be running out.

2. How does a forgotten event (recorded back in 2:21-23) suddenly become hugely significant (6:1-3)?

3. How might you have felt if, like Mordecai, your act of loyalty to the king had been ignored? Or if you knew that a gallows had been prepared for you by a powerful enemy?

Apply

4. Read Psalm 31:15; Acts 1:7. What can we learn from the timing of the king's discovery of Mordecai's loyalty?

- What does this remind us about kings and rulers? (See Proverbs 21:1.)

Getting Personal | OPTIONAL

Are there disappointments from your past that still give you pain? Or situations right now that cause you to be anxious?

What have you learned so far in these studies that can help you overcome such disappointment and anxiety?

Explore More | OPTIONAL

There are no such things as coincidences in the Bible, and God's timing is never accidental.

Read Romans 5:6

- How was this true in the past?

Read 1 Corinthians 4:5

- How will this be true in the future?

However, this is not the view of the world around us!

Read 2 Peter 3:3-12

- Where do non-believers go wrong (v 3-7)?
- What must we understand, to avoid falling into the same unbelief?
  - v 8
  - v 9
  - v 10
- When we trust in God's perfect timing, what difference does it make in our lives (v 11-12)?

Investigate

5. Reread Esther 6:6-9. What do these verses show us about Haman?

6. What do his advisers and wife recognise in verse 13? How does this differ from 5:14?

- As Haman is rushed off to Esther's second banquet, how do you think his expectations and feelings might have changed since the first one?

Read Esther 7

DICTIONARY

Covered Haman's face (v 8): a sign that he was to be put to death.

7. Describe Esther's speech in verses 3-4.

- From verse 5, why do you think Esther can now be confident that Xerxes is on her side?

8. How does Xerxes react? Why do you think he goes out into the palace garden?

9. How does Haman respond (v 6-8), and how is his fate sealed (v 8-10)?

Apply

10. How can these chapters help our faith in God to grow? (Proverbs 19:21 might help you.)

11. Read Matthew 10:17-20, 28. How are the lessons of this session reinforced by Jesus' teaching to his disciples about persecution?

    - How can these lessons help us when we face opposition for following Jesus Christ?

Getting Personal | OPTIONAL

In what ways are you tempted right now to fear people rather than God? What steps do you need to take to build trust in him for those situations?

Pray

Praise God for the specific things you have learned about him in this session.

Remind yourselves of the prayers he has answered recently and give thanks to him.

Pray for challenging things that you are facing in the coming week—for his will to be done so that his name will be glorified.

7

A Great Deliverance

Esther 8 - 10

The Story So Far...

God's people, exiled in Persia, face total destruction through the scheming of powerful Haman. But the new queen, Esther—a Jew—is able to speak courageously to the king on behalf of her people.

God times events so that, just as Haman is about to implement his plan to destroy Mordecai, the king learns that Mordecai had previously saved his life. Haman's downfall comes swiftly when Esther exposes his plot against the Jews. Humility and reliance on God are vindicated, and human pride ends in ruin.

Talkabout

1. Describe a time in your life when you thought you had completed a challenge but then found another one ahead. How did it feel?

Investigate

Read Esther 8

Esther has overcome one hurdle but the main problem is unresolved: Haman has been eliminated but his edict against the Jews still remains, a fact that the king appears to have overlooked.

2. How are Esther and Mordecai honoured after the king's fury has subsided (v 1-2)?

   - Why is this an encouraging sign?

3. Why is it still difficult (and even dangerous) for Esther to make a second request of the king, do you think? (See 4:11.)

   - What do you think motivates her and gives her courage?

4. How is the situation dealt with (v 9-14)? What shows how God has completely turned the situation around?
   - v 9—compare 3:12

   - v 10—compare 3:10, 12b

   - v 11-14—compare 3:13-15

5. What do you notice about the celebrations in verses 15-17?

6. What is the impact of these events on people of other nationalities? (Compare verse 17 with Isaiah 65:1.)

Apply

7. Read Luke 19:10; Romans 6:23; Acts 2:21. What is the great deliverance all Christians have experienced?

    - What other parallels can you see between this part of the story of Esther and the gospel?

8. For what reasons can Christians sometimes fail to respond to God's deliverance with joy, gladness and celebration?

- What impact can we have on others when they witness the effects of this good news in our lives?

Getting Personal | OPTIONAL

Honestly assess your attitude and response towards God's deliverance in your own life. How does this impact your worship both in church and throughout the week? What will help you to become more grateful and responsive?

Investigate

Read Esther 9:1-17

Esther 9:1 sums up this section: "On this day the enemies of the Jews had hoped to overpower them, but now the tables were turned and the Jews got the upper hand over those who hated them."

9. From verses 1-17, what things happened to make this possible?

Explore More | OPTIONAL

Read 2 Corinthians 10:3-5

The apostle Paul is telling us about the fight that followers of Jesus are to be engaged in. What does he say about...

- the battle?
- the enemy?
- the weapons? (See also Ephesians 6:17.)
- the aim?

Apply

10. In 1 Timothy 6:12 the apostle Paul tells us to "fight the good fight of the faith". What is involved in doing this, do you think?

- Read 2 Timothy 2:1-6, and then complete the following in your own words: A good soldier...

Getting Personal | OPTIONAL

Think carefully about whether you treat the church as a hotel, a hospital or an army. How willing are you to be involved in this battle and to fight this good fight? Are there any areas of your life where you have given up the battle?

Investigate

Read Esther 9:17 – 10:3

DICTIONARY

Lot (v 24): an object used to make a decision, like dice.

---

11. How did the Jews respond to victory (9:17-19)?

- Why did Mordecai (v 20-22) and Esther (v 29) act as they did?

Apply

We too need to remind ourselves regularly of God's goodness to us, and to ensure that we pass on the truth of the gospel to future generations.

12. Share some practical things that we can do to help each other in this (individually, in families and as churches).

Pray

Both as a group and on your own:

- *Thank God for the deliverance and victory that is in Christ.*
- *Praise him for the privilege of fighting the good fight of faith and for the rest that his people will enjoy in eternity.*
- *Pray that God will help you to fight valiantly, holding on to his promises.*

Esther

Royal Rescue

Leader's Guide: Introduction

This Leader's Guide includes guidance for every question. It will provide background information and help you if you get stuck. For each session, you'll also find the following:

The Big Idea: The main point of the session, in brief. This is what you should be aiming to have fixed in people's minds by the end of the session!

Summary: An overview of the passage you're reading together.

Optional Extra: Usually this is an introductory activity that ties in with the main theme of the Bible study and is designed to break the ice at the beginning of a session. Or it may be a "homework project" that people can tackle during the week.

Occasionally the Leader's Guide includes an extra follow-up question, printed in ***italics***. This doesn't appear in the main study guide but could be a useful add-on to help your group get to the answer or go deeper.

Here are a few key principles to bear in mind as you prepare to lead:

- Don't just read out the answers from the Leader's Guide. Ideally, you want the group to discover these answers from the Bible for themselves.
- Keep drawing people back to the passage you're studying. People may come up with answers based on their experiences or on teaching they've heard in the past, but the point of this study is to listen to God's word itself—so keep directing your group to look at the text.
- Make sure everyone finishes the session knowing how the passage is relevant for them. We do Bible study so that our lives can be changed by what we hear from God's word. So, **Apply** questions aren't just an add-on—they're a vital part of the session.

Finally, remember that your group is unique! You should feel free to use this Good Book Guide in a way that works for them. If they're a quiet bunch, you might want to spend longer on the **Talkabout** question. If they love to get creative, try using mind-mapping or doodling to kick-start some of your discussions. If your time is limited, you can choose to skip **Explore More** or split the whole session into two. Adapt the material in whatever way you think will help your group get the most out of God's word.

1

Party Time at the Palace

Esther 1

The Big Idea

People now are the same as in Esther's day—in rebellion against God, and suffering the consequences. But God is also the same—sovereign and always faithful to his promises.

Summary

Esther 1 introduces us to the Persian Empire and its ruler, King Xerxes (or Ahasuerus in Hebrew). Three lavish celebrations are arranged. But when the king commands his queen to show off her beauty to his male guests, he is refused. Fearful of the signal her insubordination will send to the nation, Xerxes deposes and banishes her. A decision is made to replace her with someone more worthy; a new decree states that every husband is to be ruler of his own home.

This session highlights the similarities between people in Esther 1 and people everywhere and throughout history—living in rebellion against God and suffering the consequences. But God is also the same—sovereign and faithful to his promises.

The exiled Jews, however, captive under the apparently invincible Persian Empire, must have sometimes doubted God's sovereignty and faithfulness, and been tempted to integrate into Persian culture. Christians today also live "in exile" in a world powerfully opposed to God, his people and his word. This session challenges us to remain the distinctive people of God, trusting that he is sovereign and faithful to his promises.

Optional Extra

Have a party to kick off this series in Esther—anything from a pizza to an elaborate dinner.

Get everyone to bring something special to "show off" to the group (e.g. a painting, jewellery, music, a medal or trophy, a book, etc.), and let them explain briefly why it's special to them.

Guidance for Questions

1. **What words would you use to describe 21st-century culture?**
   This question aims to pinpoint characteristics of our own culture so that similarities with Persian culture can be noted, highlighting the relevance of Esther's message to us. Only one or two-word answers are needed. Include positive as well as negative aspects. Possible answers: wealth, materialism, celebrity culture, drugs and alcohol, medical and educational advances, multiculturalism, religious tolerance/intolerance, sexual immorality, obsession with entertainment, opportunities for travel, etc.

2. **What do we learn about the Persian ruler, King Xerxes, and his empire?**
He was wealthy and powerful, in the third year of his reign. We see pride, generosity and extravagance as he showcases the wealth of the nation. His queen is called Vashti and they are based at the royal fortress in Susa (in modern-day Iran). He seems a generous, liberal and attentive host. His empire is vast, prosperous and powerful, with a sophisticated system of government. It covers 127 provinces from India to Cush (Ethiopia) (v 1). The long guest list of the first banquet shows that it's politically well-organised and governed. Verses 7-8 suggest the people enjoyed a good party with a steady supply of alcohol.

    NOTE: Use an atlas to show people the extent of this empire.

3. **Three celebrations are mentioned. What was the purpose of each?**
All these parties illustrate the king's sense of security and self-satisfaction. Confident in his wealth and power, he is enjoying his achievements and prestige. Everything visible in the Persian Empire seems to support this view.

- **Party 1 (v 3-4)**
For the influential leaders throughout the empire. It lasted six months, probably due to the numbers needing hospitality, and the long distances travelled. It's unlikely all the leaders in an area could come at once, because this would leave the province ungoverned. It was probably a time of consolidation, team building and preparation for future military action.

- **Party 2 (v 5-8)**
A smaller and more personal affair for the entire male palace staff. It was probably a time of relaxation after the pressure of the previous six months. It lasted only a week but the king spared no expense to show his appreciation of those who worked closest to him.

- **Party 3 (v 9)**
Held exclusively for the women and arranged by Vashti herself.

4. **Xerxes seems very proud of his rule and his kingdom. By contrast, what was the attitude of Israel's greatest ruler, King David? Read 1 Chronicles 29:10-13.**
David reminds us that the Lord is sovereign—he gives riches, honour and power at his discretion.

    NOTE: David had ruled Israel approximately 500 years earlier.

- **The Jewish prophet Isaiah lived before the Babylonian conquest and Jewish exile. What did Isaiah specifically prophesy about Cyrus (founder of the Persian Empire) in Isaiah 45:1-7, 12-13?**
That Cyrus would be God's instrument, chosen to fulfil God's righteous purposes and the good of his people. Throughout the book of Esther we will see God continuing to work out his righteous purposes, now partly through Xerxes.

NOTE (before tackling question 5): If people know little about Israel's history, you may want to outline briefly how the Jews have arrived at this point in history. Mention…

- Israel's origins in God's promises to Abraham (Genesis 12:1-3).
- how God fulfilled those promises by making them a great nation and bringing them into the land he had promised them.
- God's covenant with Israel—he would be their God, protecting and providing for them: they were to be his people, listening to his word and following his laws.
- how Israel's continual disobedience and rejection of God finally led to the break-up of the kingdom, defeat by their enemies and this exile.

5. **Imagine yourselves in the shoes of God's people, the Jews, living in exile in Persia at this time. How do you think they might feel?**
It's likely most felt homesickness and despair about returning home. Those who'd forgotten prophecies like Isaiah's (see question 4) perhaps also struggled with disappointment towards God: when God's people are captive and exiled under the apparently invincible Persian Empire, who is in control and whose purposes are being fulfilled?

- **What would make it difficult for them to remain the distinctive people of God, do you think?**
With little faith that God is willing or able to defeat the Persian superpower, and thus little hope of return to their own land and nation, the Jews might be tempted to make the best of their situation by becoming more Persian, enjoying the pleasures of Persian society.

6. **Read Philippians 3:20 and 1 Peter 2:11. In what sense are true Christians living in exile?**
    - Philippians 3:20: "Our citizenship is in heaven". That is where we belong—not in this world. We should not put down roots in this life or look to this world for fulfilment and happiness.
    - 1 Peter 2:11: We are "foreigners and exiles" in the world. We should expect to be different from others around us; we don't share their values or their ways.

- **How is the experience of being a Christian in our world similar to the experience of the Jews living in the Persian Empire of King Xerxes?**
Christians lack power and influence in our world—in the West Christians are numerically insignificant, while in the developing world Christians tend to come from the poorer sections of society. And just as the Jews lived under the apparently unbreakable power of the Persians, so this world is under the control of the evil one. (See 1 John 5:19.)

- **What makes it difficult for us to be the distinctive people of God?**
We are hated and despised for being different. We are continually tempted

to become like the rest of the world so we can enjoy their approval and join in with their pleasures.

7. **What more do we learn about Xerxes here?**
Xerxes reveals a more sinister side as he demonstrates a lack of self-control. We see him half drunk, eager to impress his guests (by showing off his wife and by demonstrating his power when his pride is wounded). He is insensitive, unreasonable, petty and petulant. Perhaps because of advisers telling him what he wants to hear rather than what is right, he ends up sacrificing his wife and the mother of his child.

- ***OPTIONAL: What specific sins do you think King Xerxes fell into or encouraged?***
Focus on those issues raised by your group or those which you think are most relevant.
    - *Drunkenness (v 10)—this is a destructive sin that often leads to sexual immorality and depravity (Proverbs 31:4-5; 23:29-35).*
    - *Pride (showing off) (v 11)—this brings a man down (Proverbs 29:23) and is something that God hates (Proverbs 8:13).*
    - *Sexual immorality—see Proverbs 5:3-10. Jesus tells us that even looking lustfully at someone who is not our marriage partner means we are guilty of adultery.*
    - *Anger (v 12)—see Proverbs 14:17a; 29:22a. A hot temper leads to disputing, sinfulness and foolishness.*

8. **Who does he blame for the crisis that follows his wife's refusal to comply with his command? (See verse 15.)**
Vashti, for not paying due respect to him even though the proper etiquette was used (v 15b)!

- **Do you think he was justified in deposing the queen? Who or what else could be responsible for this humiliating situation?**
These questions are open to interpretation but should lead to an interesting discussion. Many commentators believe Xerxes wanted his wife to appear naked or semi-dressed. History also indicates the birth of Vashti's son, Artaxerxes, around this time. The New Testament's teaching on marriage shows that God expects husbands to cherish their wives—something Xerxes failed in badly. So it's possible to make the case that Xerxes was wrong both to expect his wife to go on public display and to react as he did when she refused. But the book of Esther makes no comment on this.

9. **What was the ripple effect of this incident, both personally and nationally?**
Xerxes lost his wife; Vashti lost her home, position and place in society; Persia lost their queen; and probably wives across the empire lost some freedom.

Explore More

- ***Read Ephesians 2:1-3; Philippians 3:18-19; Colossians 3:5-10; 1 Peter 4:1-4. What are the behaviour and cultures of the world like, according to the New Testament apostles?***
  - *Ephesians 2:1-3: Dead in sins (v 1); following the devil ("the ruler of the kingdom of the air") and disobedient to God (v 2); gratifying the cravings of the flesh (v 3).*
  - *Philippians 3:18-19: Living as enemies of the cross of Christ; putting their appetites first; glorying in things that should make them ashamed.*
  - *Colossians 3:5-10: Idolising sexual immorality, evil desires, greed; full of anger, lies, filthy language.*
  - *1 Peter 4:1-4: Living in debauchery, lust, drunkenness and idolatry; abusing those who don't join in.*
- ***What drives them to be like this?***
  Getting what they want. This makes them disobedient to God, followers of the devil, and enemies of the cross of Christ.
- ***Is this how we see our society?***
  Challenge your group to see our culture in this way, and not as morally neutral.
- ***How will God's people (true Christians) stand out?***
  They won't join in with this way of life, and therefore will be persecuted for being different (1 Peter 4:4).

10. **There are many similarities between Persian culture and our own culture today. Briefly identify some of the specific problems that we, our families and our churches face, living as God's people in a secular culture.**
This question highlights the fallen nature of our world, and the truth that Christians must battle against sin both in their own hearts and in society.

Problems for Christians include: hostility towards Christian teaching; negative perceptions of Christians; the silencing and ridiculing of Christian values; state intervention that attempts to regulate Christian activity and provokes conscientious law-breaking by Christians; the promotion of values opposed to God's word in education, culture and popular entertainment, etc.

All these can undermine our confidence in the Bible; what we teach to Christians and non-Christians; our efforts to build relationships with non-Christians; our level of involvement in wider society. The upshot is that we are constantly pressured to fit in with the non-Christians around us.

Let your discussion be shaped by the experiences of Christians in your group.

- **Read 1 Corinthians 6:9-11. What hope does the gospel bring?**
  Jesus took the judgment we deserved upon himself on the cross. This means we are cleansed, made right in God's sight and are being

changed to become like his Son, and heirs of the kingdom of God. It's this hope that equips and empowers Christians to keep on being the distinctive people of God.

11. **In this session we have seen the consequences of Xerxes' drunkenness: pride and showing off; petulant, uncontrolled anger; and blame-shifting. When Christians fall into sinful behaviours like those of Xerxes, how does it affect those around us?**
When Christians fall into sinful behaviour, they look no different from the non-Christians around them. Fellow Christians who are struggling to stay distinctive are weakened and discouraged, and our witness to non-Christians is compromised.

- **Read James 4:6-10. What do we need to do when we fall into these kinds of sins?**
Humble ourselves before the Lord (v 6, 7, 10), which involves repentance, going to the cross for forgiveness, and prayerful dependence on the Holy Spirit. Accountability to other Christians who can encourage and correct us is helpful.

2

Waiting in the Wings

Esther 2

The Big Idea

Although God is not mentioned in this chapter by name, we see his presence and guidance through people and circumstances.

Summary

The search begins for a new queen. The most beautiful young women are brought to the royal harem, where they undergo intense beauty therapy. Esther (a Jewess and the lovely adopted daughter of Mordecai) is one of many put under the care of the royal official, Hegai. He favours her and the year ends with the king choosing her as his wife. Throughout this part of the story, Mordecai, who seems to have a job at the palace, keeps a discreet but watchful eye on Esther and even prevents an assassination attempt on Xerxes.

In this session we see God's faithfulness and continuing presence with his people in the successful outcome of events for Esther and the "coincidences" experienced by Mordecai. Both Esther and Mordecai shine out as people of God—their godly characters of integrity, wisdom and humility stand in stark contrast to the vanity and obsession with merely physical beauty that characterise Persian culture.

This session examines how Christians are to be distinctive in attitudes to physical appearance. We also see how God uses everything, including the sin of his enemies, to further his purposes. And we are reminded of God's continual loving presence with his people in all situations.

Optional Extra

(For women) A make-up/beauty-product or beautician/hairdresser demo.

(For young people) Construct a quiz; divide the group into two teams; choose a representative for each team. If a team gets their question right, they have to dress up their representative and put make-up/hair product/perfume on them.

Guidance for Questions

1. **Describe a time and situation when you felt extremely uncomfortable and out of place. How did it turn out?**
   This question is meant to develop a sensitivity to how Esther would have felt after being transported into a situation completely alien to her.

2. **What is so appealing to Xerxes about the advice of the royal attendants, do you think?**
   History tells us that Xerxes had expected to win the war against the Greeks so it's likely that he was feeling despondent, vulnerable and isolated. Perhaps this was his advisors' attempt to cheer him up. Although he had the choice of many women, perhaps he missed the intimacy and stability of a wife. The selection process itself is likely to have appealed too.

   - **How does this fit with what we learned about him in session 1?**
     We've already seen that Xerxes was a vain and proud man, so it's likely that he felt a beautiful queen would enhance his image and prestige in the eyes of himself and others.

3. **Read Proverbs 31:10-11, 30. Compare the qualities that were thought to be most desirable in a new queen with those that are most valued by God.**
   Each candidate was to be both young and a virgin. To be successful she needed to charm the king with her beauty and sexual prowess. However, Proverbs 31:10-11 reveals the foolishness of this—physical beauty is only temporary and, when accompanied merely by charm, very deceptive, covering ugliness of character like a mask. Beauty of character is far less common than physical beauty but much more valuable, satisfying and enriching.

4. **In which ways does our society share "Persian values" when it comes to physical appearance? What problems can this create for us (whether we're male or female)?**
   This could spark a helpful discussion. Many negative issues in our society can be highlighted (celebrity culture,

eating disorders, pornography, sexual permissiveness, spending on cosmetic surgery and image-enhancing goods, etc.) but there may be other issues worth exploring too.

For young or single people: Think about the group's criteria for choosing friendships and developing relationships. For example, what to look for in a potential partner. What kind of people are you drawn to at school, church, university? Do they have to look a certain way for you to befriend them? Or to feel part of your group? Do you feel you have to look a certain way to fit in?

For a men's/boys' group: You could discuss how to handle the huge amount of sexual imagery they are bombarded with on billboards, TV, internet, in magazines, etc.

For women and teenagers: Discuss the pressures they feel as a result of their own or others' expectations.

- **Read 1 Samuel 16:7. How are Christians to be different on this issue of physical appearance?**
  Christians are to be like God, who is not impressed or swayed by outward appearance but instead focuses on what goes on in our hearts.

- **Read 1 Peter 3:3-4. How can we help each other to live by God's values?**
  Instead of looking to fashion and image, we should aim to be beautiful by cultivating "a gentle and quiet spirit"—a spirit that trusts in God rather than battling to promote ourselves and our interests. Discuss practically how Christians can help each other to think like this. What do we compliment each other about—looks or character? Do we have strong, loving relationships in which we challenge each other and are challenged?

5. **What do we learn about Mordecai and Esther?**
   - Mordecai has good Jewish credentials. He is a Benjamite and his great-grandfather, Kish, was exiled from Jerusalem by the Babylonians. He is a compassionate man, shown by the adopting of his young cousin after the death of her parents.
   - She is called Esther and her beauty is emphasised in verse 7. Esther is her Persian name, which means "star". Her Jewish name is Hadassah, which means "fragrance". She follows the instructions of those who care for her—Mordecai (v 10, 20) and Hegai (v 15).

6. **Describe the experiences that Esther went through in verses 8-18. Would it have been an exciting adventure or a terrifying ordeal? Why do you think that?**
   - v 8: Esther was taken and placed into the harem under the care of Hegai.
   - v 9: Hegai liked her from the start, so gave her special food, beauty treatments, accommodation along with seven maids.
   - v 12: She had a year of beauty treatment.

- v 16: She spent a night with the king.
- v 17: The king chose her, crowned her, held a party and declared a holiday, and gave gifts generously in her honour.

In discussing this question, there are certain things worth bearing in mind. Verse 8 makes clear there was a royal command to round up the most beautiful women in the kingdom. It is unlikely therefore that Esther or her guardian, Mordecai, had any choice in the matter. When she was taken into the care of the eunuch in charge of the harem, many things would have been alien to Esther—court life, living in a harem run by a eunuch, being given seven maids, being honoured and pampered, being sexually educated and prepared for a night with Xerxes, who had a dubious track record when it came to looking after a wife. She was separated from her family, with no prospect of returning to her old way of life or living a normal family life with a husband and children in the future. Culturally and religiously, there would have been many differences from her life with Mordecai.

- **Why do you think Mordecai forbade Esther to reveal her nationality and family background (v 10)?**

The reasons for this secrecy will become clear in Esther 3. But given what we have already learned about God's people in exile in a pagan culture, it's likely that some people will already have a good idea why both Esther and Mordecai keep quiet about their racial origin.

7. **Read Genesis 39:2-5, 20-23. Although God is not mentioned, how can we see that he is with Esther?**

God shows Esther he is with her both through people and circumstances. Hegai favours Esther from the beginning. She is therefore spared some considerable discomfort by being given extra privileges and care, and by being moved to live in the best place in the harem. Verse 15 tells us that everyone who saw her liked her. The fact that the king chose her as queen at the end of the year saved her from the humiliation of living as a concubine for the remainder of her life. Mordecai was also faithful to her and he continued to demonstrate his concern by advising her. She can be compared to Joseph—we are told that God was with him even in jail, giving him success in everything he did. (See Explore More below.)

8. **How does Proverbs 21:1 relate to Esther 2:17?**

Xerxes' feelings and decisions are ultimately directed by God.

Explore More

- ***Look at the following Bible events and discuss how each reveals God's complete sovereignty over evil.***

NOTE: If people do not know these stories, briefly outline each one instead of seeking answers to the questions below.

- ***Genesis 50:18-20: How did God use the hatred of Joseph's brothers towards Joseph for the benefit of his people?***
  Joseph's brothers intended to harm him when they sold him into slavery and he was taken to Egypt, but when God helped him to become a great leader there, Joseph played a vital role in rescuing his family from famine in their homeland.

- ***Exodus 5:1-8, 19-22; 6:1-7: How did God use the furious refusal of Pharaoh to obey his word for the benefit of his people?***
  Pharaoh intended to show his contempt for God and his power over God's people, but God changed this into an opportunity to show Israel and the world his far greater power as he rescued Israel from Egypt with many great signs and wonders. His purpose was that his people would truly know who he was.

- ***Acts 2:22-24: How did God use the hatred of the Jewish leaders towards Jesus to benefit his people?***
  The Jewish leaders planned to do away with Jesus once and for all by having him executed on a cross, but God had planned from before creation that the cross of Jesus would be the means by which sinners can be saved (Colossians 1:20).

- ***What can we learn from these true stories that will help us in times when evil seems to be winning over good?***
  Christians will be greatly helped by understanding how God works out his purposes and that he often allows hardship so that his power and sovereignty will be displayed all the more clearly.

---

9. **Esther was separated from her family and people. Give examples of periods of isolation and change that we sometimes face. When might we feel isolated because we are Christians?**
   - E.g. moving home, area, country, church, job; leaving home to go to university; loneliness in school; bereavement and divorce; unemployment; physical and mental illness and times in hospital; singleness.
   - We might feel isolated when we are the only Christian in the family, office, etc.

- **Why do you think Christians often struggle in their faith at these times? On the other hand, how can these experiences be a blessing?**
  - These can be dangerous times as we struggle with the lack of fellowship and support that have encouraged us in the past. Potential dangers include: general discouragement; the desire to fit in at the expense of obedience to Christ; and becoming trapped by the things that the world says are important. (See 1 John 2:15.)

- However these are opportunities for our faith, obedience and reliance on God to grow, deepening our experience of and relationship with him. Onlookers learn of God's faithfulness to his people in hard times and are encouraged to trust him, bringing further glory to God. (See 2 Corinthians 1:3-7 for a real-life example.)

- **Read John 10:29 and Romans 8:31-33, 38-39. What assurances do these verses give us, no matter what we're experiencing?**
  God has promised never to leave or forsake us. In John 10:29, Jesus himself tells us that God, who is much more powerful than anyone or anything else, has a firm hold of us. Romans 8:38-39 reminds us that it's impossible for absolutely anything or anyone to separate us from his love because, as verses 31-33 affirm, he paid the ultimate price for us. So it's completely ridiculous to think he would ever dream of letting us go or deny us anything we need to live for him.

10. **Is it possible to prepare ourselves in advance for such challenges? How?**
    In one sense we can never be fully prepared for the impact these experiences will have on our lives, but we can take every opportunity to feed ourselves on God's word with prayer and fellowship so that we are strong when trials come. However, God is always prepared. We can often look back on our lives and see how he has quietly prepared us in advance for the things he knows will happen. He also promises us that his grace is sufficient for all our needs. See 2 Corinthians 12:9-10.

11. **What evidence is there in this chapter that Mordecai is a man of integrity, love and wisdom?**
    Notice Mordecai's attitude to Esther (already mentioned in question 5)—adopting her (v 7), advising her wisely (v 20), checking up on her daily (v 11), thus showing her loyalty and ongoing care. He manages to save the king's life by uncovering an assassination, the details of which he passes to the king through Esther.

12. **Read 1 Peter 3:3-4. How does Esther show the true inner beauty that God values?**
    Esther demonstrates humility in her response to advice given by Hegai (v 15) and also Mordecai (v 10), despite her meteoric social rise. She does not accept any praise for revealing the assassination conspiracy but rather gives all the credit to Mordecai (v 22). She gains Hegai's favour very quickly and the king chooses her as his queen. This would suggest that there was something special, not only in her physical beauty but also in her character and demeanour. Again, there is a strong resemblance to the story of Joseph, who was favoured in both Potiphar's household and later in prison (Genesis 39:2-5, 21-23).

3

The Gathering Storm

Esther 3

The Big Idea

There is great conflict between God and Satan, often resulting in extreme persecution of God's people; yet, despite appearances, God remains sovereign.

Summary

When Haman is made prime minister, a royal order commands everyone to bow down and honour him. Mordecai repeatedly refuses despite pressure from others. When Haman realises this, he not only plots revenge on Mordecai but takes steps to destroy all Jews.

This is more than merely sinful racism; it's part of a pattern that is repeated throughout history—the outworking on earth of the hostility of Satan and his agents (both humans and spirits) towards God. It is seen in the violent and unreasonable hatred of God's enemies towards his people—the Jews in the Old Testament and the church in the New Testament—and, ultimately, towards Jesus Christ. The story of Esther is part of Satan's attempt to prevent the birth of Jesus Christ (Revelation 12:4). Satan's goal to destroy God's Messiah culminated in Christ's death on the cross. Paradoxically though, this "moment of triumph" for God's enemy was actually the means by which Satan has been defeated for ever (Hebrews 2:14-15; Revelation 12:5, 7-8, 10-11).

This session investigates the characteristics and strategies of God's enemies, and the godly response to their opposition—seen here in Mordecai—which is to stand firm as one of God's people. We see why Christians are called to suffer, and how we can be helped and encouraged to stand firm ourselves.

Optional Extra

Alongside the theme of opposition to God and his people, you could show a video or use articles to highlight the plight of persecuted Christians today. (Organisations such as Barnabas Fund, Open Doors, and Release International provide good resources.)

Guidance for Questions

1. **Who do you think are the opponents of God's people today?**
   Answers could include: secular humanists and "evangelising" atheists; some sects of other religions, especially where anti-Western; those who have bought into political correctness; those with "liberal" standards of morality and ethics; hedonists, etc. Some people may point out that the true enemies of Christians today are in fact the powers of evil that work through these human opponents. (See Ephesians 6:12; also question 4.)

- **How do they show their opposition?**
  Focus on what is currently in the news. Human opposition is seen in lawsuits against Christians because of their beliefs; employment codes that restrict Christians' freedom of expression; attacks in the media; debates over what is and isn't allowed in schools; protests about Christian events or buildings; preferential treatment of other religions, etc. Spiritual opposition works through these events.

2. **In chapter 3:10 Haman is called "the enemy of the Jews". Look at verses 1-6. What are the first signs of this?**
   - The writer is careful to note Haman's family credentials, revealing why he hated the Jews so much. (See the dictionary in the Study Guide.) Haman was an Amalekite of Agag's tribe. After the Israelites left Egypt, the Amalekites attacked them in the desert, yet suffered a humiliating defeat (Exodus 17:8-16). Centuries later, the Amalekites, under King Agag, fought against King Saul the Benjamite (Mordecai's tribe). This conflict ended with the execution of King Agag at the hands of Samuel (1 Samuel 15:32-33).
   - Verse 4 makes it clear that the officials knew that Haman had a problem with the Jews. Because Mordecai was a Jew, they waited to see if his behaviour would be tolerated or condemned.
   - Mordecai seems to have used his nationality as the reason why he wouldn't bow, therefore showing that he too knew of Haman's problem with the Jews.

- **How could this enmity help to explain 2:10 and 20?**
  As Haman's political career and royal approval was on the rise in chapter 2, this is most likely the reason for Mordecai advising Esther to keep her nationality a secret.

3. **In verses 1-5, what are the signs that Mordecai is a man of principle and courage?**
   Mordecai refuses to bow to Haman, not once but repeatedly ("day after day"—v 4), despite the pressure put upon him by others in authority (v 3), the dangerous consequences he risks (v 6), and the fact that it seems he alone stands when the crowd bows (v 2). He is also honest about his nationality and faith (v 4b)—something that up to now he has kept secret in the palace environment.

- **What drives Mordecai's behaviour, do you think? And what has no effect on his behaviour?**
  Mordecai demonstrates a fear of God which is far greater than any fear of man. He is determined not to give honour to a man who is an enemy of God's people, and therefore of God himself. Haman's power and importance has no effect on Mordecai's behaviour.

- **How do we know that he isn't a rebel against the king? (See 2:21-22.)**
  Mordecai is not generally insubordinate. He has shown respect for the authority of Xerxes, even foiling an assassination attempt. (See end of chapter 2.)

4. **Read Ephesians 6:10-13. What more does this tell us about the enemies of God's people today?**
   God's people are in a battle not just with people who don't have the same beliefs or outlook as we do. Rather, there is a spiritual element as Satan himself rages against God and his people. It is he who is behind the persecution and conflict we face.

- **What two strategies do God's enemies use against his people? (See verses 11 and 13. Hint: think about what the "day of evil" is.)**
  - v 11: "The devil's schemes" suggests deception and manipulation of people.
  - v 13: "The day of evil", when Christians will need the "full armour of God" to stand their ground, suggests a direct attack—most likely outright persecution.

5. **Why do we often find it difficult to take a stand and remain firm?**
   Because we are human and Satan knows how to attack our weak spots. To stand firm needs courage, discipline and energy, something we often struggle with. We too easily rely on our own limited strength rather than on the power that is ours through the Holy Spirit. Sometimes, too, our fear of other people is greater than our respect for God.

- **Why is it important to do so?**
  Many reasons, including...
  - Our life here is temporary. Christ has actually won the spiritual battle on the cross and will return one day to claim that victory and finally destroy Satan. Everything will be made new and we will reign with him for eternity. This is our goal as Christians.
  - When we realise the sacrifice Jesus made for us, our response will be one of thanks and love displayed through obedience which will often be costly. Living for the honour of his name will be of huge importance.
  - Those who do not stand firm will, in the end, be destroyed (Hebrews 10:36-39).

6. **How does Haman put his plan into action?**
   - He seeks superstitious guidance (v 7).
   - He manipulates King Xerxes through lies and innuendo (v 8), exploiting the vulnerability that the king is likely to have felt after the failed assassination attempt at the end of chapter 2.
   - He shows devotion to the king by offering a substantial amount of personal cash to finance the scheme (v 9). Haman's success is proven when Xerxes not only turns this grand gesture down but expresses gratitude by placing his own signet ring on Haman's finger (v 10-11).

Xerxes shows complete trust in Haman, approving his scheme without scrutiny.

- Haman uses every power and resource available to him—scribes copy and translate his orders into every language of the empire. Haman's newly acquired signet ring is used to give the letters royal authority (v 12). They are sent by express royal delivery to the authorities in every province (v 13).
- The order given is very strong: "Destroy, kill and annihilate all the Jews—young and old, women and children—on a single day" (v 13).
- Haman gives material incentive by expressly permitting plunder of the goods of those Jews who are killed (v 13).
- The edict is copied and made law in every province, then explained to every nationality (v 14). Ignorance of this edict cannot be used as an excuse.

- **How does he reflect the devil's strategies (Ephesians 6:11 and 13)?** Haman uses a deceptive and manipulative scheme to get the king to do what he wants (v 8-12), and his ultimate goal is a murderous attack—a "day of evil"—against the entire Jewish race (v 13).

- ***OPTIONAL: Read Proverbs 21:30; 16:33. Why can we be assured that the situation is not out of God's control?***
  - *21:30: No scheme, however clever, can outwit God.*
  - *16:33: Even the casting of lots (or drawing straws / throwing dice) is controlled by God.*

7. **If Haman's plot had succeeded, how would the rest of Bible history have been affected? What would the eternal consequences have been, both for Jews and non-Jews?**
   - If the Jews had been destroyed, then there would have been no Messiah (the one chosen by God to rescue and rule his people) i.e. Jesus.
   - NOTE: If your group has little Bible knowledge, talk about how Jesus fulfils God's promises to send his Messiah (e.g. Genesis 12:3—blessing to all peoples on earth through a descendant of Abraham; Acts 3:25-26—Peter explains that Jesus (see verse 13a) is the fulfilment of God's promise to Abraham.)
   - Without Jesus coming to this world as God's Messiah, there would be no rescue from God's judgment either for Jews or non-Jews.

8. **List the character traits of Haman throughout this chapter.**
   Cruel, vengeful, proud, superstitious, manipulative, scheming, a liar and cold-hearted. An enemy of God.

- **What motivates his actions?**
  Hatred of God's people, and therefore of God.

9. **You would expect the *Jews* to be devastated, but verse 15 says that the city of Susa *as a whole* was bewildered. Why might this be**

the case, do you think? (Jeremiah 29:4-7 might help you here.)
Notice the contrast between Xerxes and Haman celebrating and the confusion in Susa. When the Jews were first exiled, the Jewish prophet, Jeremiah, had told them to be good citizens and pray for their place of exile so that their conquerors, and they themselves, would prosper. It's likely therefore that the people of Susa felt this attack on the Jews was outrageous and inexplicable.

- **What does this show us about the hostility of people like Haman towards God and his people?**
  Sinful people hate God without reason (see John 15:25), and likewise they hate God's people without reason. (See, for example, David—Psalm 35:19.)

- ***OPTIONAL: What are the implications for Christians today?***
  Sometimes, however faithfully we live for our Lord and however much we show love and do good, Christians will still be persecuted, because God's enemies hate him—and his Son and his people—without reason.

Explore More

- ***Read Revelation 12:1-10. What was the devil's goal in verse 4? Was he successful?***
  See Study Guide, page 23, for how to understand the symbolism. The devil wanted to destroy God's Messiah (the King and Rescuer promised by God) as soon as he appeared. This is seen clearly in the threat from Herod to Jesus' life soon after birth (Matthew 2:13-18).

- ***After Jesus' death, resurrection and ascension (v 5), what happened in heaven (v 7-10)?***
  There was a war in heaven. Satan and his angels were defeated.

- ***What has changed for Satan as a result of this (v 8, 10b)?***
  Satan and his angels have been evicted from heaven—they have lost the place that they had there before (e.g. Job 1:6-12), and have been thrown down to the earth.

- ***What does this passage reveal about Satan's activity in Esther's time?***
  Satan's agenda throughout the Old Testament was to destroy the Messiah (v 4b). In Esther's day, Satan was working through those, like Haman, who wanted to destroy Israel, the nation from which God had promised the Messiah would be born.

---

10. **How do these verses help us to understand why we face opposition for living as followers of Jesus?**
    - **John 15:18-25**
      Jesus was hated without reason and we will be too because we are his followers.
    - **1 Peter 4:3-4**
      People will be puzzled by the change in our lives and behaviour, often offended that we don't want to join

them in sinful practices anymore, and could even be aggressive towards us.

11. **How can we be encouraged when we face opposition? (Read 2 Corinthians 2:14-16.)**
As we live as followers of Jesus, the life-giving fragrance of the gospel is spread to those around us. Some will hate that fragrance and turn from it, (the consequence for them is "death") but others will welcome it and find life in Christ. So we shouldn't fear opposition—it's a sign that the gospel message is getting through and it will bring life to some. Our lives and words are having an effect. And far from being in danger of defeat, verse 14 assures us that we have victory in Jesus—these verses describe his "triumphal procession".

- ***OPTIONAL: Will we always face opposition, do you think?***
Christ already leads us in "triumphal procession". The enemy has been defeated (see Explore More) so opposition to God and his gospel must one day end.

12. **How could you now help a friend who is thinking of giving up the Christian faith because of opposition from friends and family?**
This question gives your group an opportunity to apply what they have learned this session about the persecution of God's people. You may like to do this as a role-play between the two friends.

4

A Challenge Set

Esther 4

The Big Idea

Fear is transformed into faith when God's sovereignty is understood and his promises are believed.

Summary

Haman's plans cause deep distress for Mordecai and all the Jews. Mordecai however remains confident that God will deliver his people (4:14).

NOTE: God has already promised that his people will return to the land of Israel at the end of 70 years in exile (Jeremiah 29:10-14).

Queen Esther meanwhile knows nothing of the crisis until Mordecai appears at the palace gates. Mordecai's faith in God's sovereignty and faithfulness to his promises leads him to persuade Esther to intervene—to risk her life and use the unique position in which God has placed her, by interceding with the king for the lives of her people.

Esther is terrified but Mordecai challenges her again. Esther requests prayer and fasting from Mordecai and the Jewish people. She decides to go to the king—she has started on the process of transformation from fear to faith.

There are two main applications for Christians.

1. The relationship between God's sovereignty and our responsibility. God sovereignly placed Esther and Mordecai in positions where they could act to fulfil his plan of rescuing the Jews. He also equipped them (with promises of his deliverance) to do that. Similarly, God brings Christians into his kingdom, where we can act to bring about his plan of rescuing the nations through the gospel of Jesus Christ, and he equips us to do that through his word.
2. Faith in God's sovereignty and faithfulness overcomes fear. This kind of faith enabled both Mordecai and Esther to act courageously in desperate and dangerous circumstances. Faith in the truths of God's word enables Christians to witness to Jesus Christ in a hostile world.

Optional Extra

Watch a performance of Spellbound (an acrobatic group who won *Britain's Got Talent* in 2010—see YouTube). Discuss what is needed for a group like this to perform such amazing feats (total faith in each other). You could also read out an excerpt about the life and faith of someone like George Müller, known for his great faith in God's provision and sovereign intervention.

NOTE: These two examples of what can be achieved through faith are both fairly spectacular. However, most ordinary Christians by definition will not achieve "extraordinary" things. So applications should emphasise our fear of doing what God wants all Christians to do—to be witnesses of Jesus Christ in a hostile world—and how faith overcomes that fear.

Guidance for Questions

1. **Think of a time when someone personally challenged you to do something that you were afraid of. Did they convince you to do it? How?**
   In chapter 4, Mordecai successfully persuades Esther to do something dangerous even though she is terrified. The aim of this question is to introduce this aspect. Some examples: trying an adventure sport, public speaking, confronting a phobia, undergoing hospital treatment, etc.

2. **Look at the Jews' reaction to the royal edict in verse 3. How would you describe their feelings?**
   There's an outpouring of grief as the news is received. The depth of distress is clear from the graphic language in verse 3. "In every province ... great mourning ... with fasting, weeping and wailing ... Many lay in sackcloth and ashes."

- ***OPTIONAL: How might they be tempted to view God at this point?***
  (NOTE: It's worth mentioning that God had already promised to deliver the Jews from exile after 70 years—see question 7 below.) Common reactions are to panic and forget about God's sovereignty altogether. Or bewilderment or anger—"How could God let this happen to us?" Or fatalism—"God is against us, and there's nothing we can do about it". These are all common reactions but ones lacking faith either in God's sovereignty or mercy.

- ***OPTIONAL: In what way would someone's trust or lack of trust in God's sovereignty be evident here?***
  Faith in God doesn't mean we don't feel distress in a situation like this. But faith in God's sovereignty and mercy makes us turn to him in repentance, reliant on his intervention. The opposite of faith is fear, which drives us away from God.

3. **To what extent do you think this crisis is Mordecai's fault?**
   At surface level, Mordecai's refusal to bow to Haman could be blamed for this crisis, yet Haman's response is completely disproportionate to Mordecai's supposed crime. As we saw in chapter 3, Haman's hatred for the Jews ran deep and was seemingly well known. Mordecai's stand was merely the excuse Haman needed to avenge himself on the Jews.

- ***OPTIONAL: Why do you think some Jews might have wanted to blame Mordecai?***
  Mordecai's refusal to bow to Haman was a courageous display of his submission to God, the King over all kings, by refusing to honour the enemy of God and his people. He showed deep faith in God's sovereignty—the sovereign God is to be

feared (i.e. honoured and obeyed) above all men, regardless of the consequences. Those who don't trust in God's sovereignty will fear men and what they can do instead. They will blame those who make a stand for God's honour because they cannot trust God over the expected consequences. Compare Daniel 3:16-18.

4. **How does Mordecai react? What does he do and where does he go (v 1-8)?**
   His grief is both immediate and public: he tears his clothes, puts on sackcloth, shakes ashes over his head and makes his way to the king's gate—"wailing loudly and bitterly"—to contact Esther.

- **How can we tell that despite his distress Mordecai still trusts in God?**
  Mordecai believes that Esther's position will help in the Jews' deliverance. But more than that, he is certain that, with or without Esther's help, the Jews will be delivered (v 14). (See also question 8.)

- ***OPTIONAL: Some people believe that grief shows lack of trust in God's sovereignty. What does Mordecai's response show us?***
  Grief over a distressing situation is not incompatible with faith. The key issue is what people do in their grief. Some turn away from God because they lack faith in him. Faith in God leads others to call out to him, to repent, or to take action because they know he will intervene—like Mordecai here.

- ***OPTIONAL (This question helps us to get into the story before we answer question 5): Put yourselves in Esther's shoes and describe the various emotions that she must have gone through in verses 4-11.***
  Initially she would be unaware of Haman's plans; then shocked at Mordecai's public mourning; she would experience fear and distress, perhaps terror, as she received Mordecai's news and his appeal for help.

5. **Esther seems afraid in verse 11. Why, do you think? (It may help to look up Esther 1:12, 19; 2:20; 3:4, 11; 4:2; and also Nehemiah 2:2.)**
   It's likely that Esther is fearful on four counts:
   - v 11: Royal etiquette designed to protect the king (probably from assassination) means that approaching the king without an invitation could result in execution. Esther knows there's one exception to this rule, but her words (end of verse 11) suggest she fears that she is out of favour. If she's right, and the king doesn't extend his sceptre, she will be killed. The fate of Vashti (Esther 1:12, 19) can't be far from her mind at this point.
   - There are also strict rules concerning mourning before the king. Mordecai didn't venture further than the palace gates (Esther 4:2). Compare Nehemiah, who took a great risk by serving wine with a

sad face to Xerxes' son, Artaxerxes (Nehemiah 2:2). Showing sadness to the king was interpreted as dissatisfaction with the king's rule. But Esther's tragic message cannot be delivered with a smile.

- The enemy of the Jews is Xerxes' new, trusted and powerful prime minister (3:4, 11). Haman is in favour, whereas Esther fears she is out of favour.
- Xerxes himself has rubber-stamped Haman's edict, while his own queen's ethnic identity and relationship with Mordecai is still a secret (2:20).

6. **When Mordecai challenges Esther in verses 13 and 14, what arguments does he use?**
   - Her royal status won't protect her (v 13).
   - If she doesn't speak to the king, then God's deliverance will come in some other way, but she and her family will be judged by God (v 14a).
   - This is probably the very reason why God put her in the position of queen in the first place (v 14b).

- **Do you think this was an easy plea to make? Why / why not?**
  Despite Mordecai's depth of feeling for Esther as her adoptive father, he asks her to risk her life—something immensely difficult for any loving parent to do. Yet he looks beyond the temporary dangers to the eternal consequences for Esther.

7. **Read Jeremiah 29:10-14. How do Mordecai's words in verse 14 line up with this message from God through the prophet Jeremiah?**
   Jeremiah 29:10-14 contains God's promises to the Jewish exiles at the beginning of their captivity. Despite their sin, they are assured of deliverance from their captors after 70 years of exile. At the time of Esther, this promised deliverance is in the process of being fulfilled and Mordecai knows it! When Mordecai states that deliverance will come, he is refusing to believe that this exile—and Haman's edict—is the end for the Jews. He is confident in God's promise to prosper, and not harm, his people. God has made his plans already and he will never change them.

8. **What do Mordecai's words in verses 13-14 tell us about...**
   This question gets people to summarise Mordecai's thinking and faith. Make sure that people understand what Mordecai is trusting in: God's sovereignty—his power over everyone and everything; and God's faithfulness—to the promises he has made to his people (e.g. Jeremiah 29:10-14). Help your group make the link between true faith in God and courageous action, like Mordecai's stand against Haman and his difficult challenge to Esther.

- **God?**
  Mordecai points out that God is sovereign over all as Judge (to whom we will all one day be accountable),

Deliverer and Ordainer. He can also be trusted to keep his promises—"relief and deliverance for the Jews will arise" (v 14).

- **Mordecai's own faith?**
  His assured words here indicate a robust faith rooted in a sound understanding of God. This is not just head knowledge! His courage before Haman in chapter 3 has already shown that he practises what he preaches.

- **Mordecai's relationship with Esther?**
  Much as he loves her, this love is clearly secondary to his fear of God. He does not gloss over the truth of her position. He courageously challenges her to take seriously her eternal future and present responsibilities. Mordecai's words might seem harsh; yet they reveal a deep love for Esther, enriched by his fear of God.

9. **What does verse 14b suggest about the relationship between God's sovereignty and our responsibility? (See also Jeremiah 1:4-7.)**
   God has sovereignly made Esther queen, but she now has to act. This shows that although God doesn't need our obedience to accomplish his will, he does choose to use us. In Jeremiah 1:4-5, God says that he created Jeremiah and knew him in the womb, sovereignly appointing Jeremiah as his prophet. Jeremiah's responsibility was then to live out his calling by speaking God's message to the nations (v 6-7).

10. **Read Ephesians 2:8-10. How does the answer to question 9 relate to our salvation?**
    We have faith and salvation only through God sovereignly pouring out his grace on us. Yet he has given us new life in Christ for the purpose of doing the specific good works that he has carefully planned for us to do. Doing these good works is our responsibility—not as a duty, however, but as a privilege.

- **Read 2 Timothy 3:16-17. How does God equip all Christians today for "good works"?**
  It is through the word of God that every Christian is "thoroughly equipped for every good work". Because Mordecai knew and trusted in God's word about deliverance from the exile (e.g. Jeremiah 29:10-14), he made the most of his God-given opportunity—both knowing about Haman's plot and able to influence Esther—to do the "good work" of challenging and persuading Esther.

- **So, what are the "good works" that have been prepared in advance for us to do (Ephesians 2:10)?**
  2 Timothy 3:16-17 shows that good works spring from obedience to God's word. This needs to be worked out in our specific situations, and results in holy living.

Explore More

- ***Read Revelation 12:9-12, 17. What was the devil doing in heaven, which he can no longer do (v 10)?***
  He was accusing God's people before God. In other words he was pointing out to God the sins of those whom God loved, which rightly meant that God must punish them with eternal death. He can no longer do this because of the life, death, resurrection and ascension of Jesus Christ (v 5). Jesus suffered God's judgment on sin and those who trust in him (Christians) receive Jesus' righteousness (2 Corinthians 5:21). Christians are now blameless and holy in God's sight and Satan's accusations are worthless.
- ***Where is the devil now and what is he doing (v 12, 17)?***
  The devil knows he has been defeated by the cross of Christ and is filled with fury (v 12). He is allowed to continue operating in this world and so he vents his fury on Christians (v 17).
- ***How do God's people (Christians) now continue to fight against him (v 11)?***
  Christians overcome the devil by "the blood of the Lamb"—the message that the death of Jesus on the cross rescues his people from God's judgment on sin. And by "the word of their testimony"—Christians telling people that they follow Christ and what he has done for them. Notice that in doing this, Christians sometimes lose their lives (end of verse 11).
- ***What is life in this world now like for God's people (v 17, see also verse 11b)?***
  It can be tough and frightening because Satan is making war on Christians, and some of them will die for their testimony about Christ. Our experiences will sometimes be similar to those of Mordecai and Esther.
- ***Overall, is this passage encouraging or discouraging? Why?***
  Encouraging because, despite his fury against God's people, Satan has been defeated by Jesus' death on the cross. (See also Hebrews 2:14-15.) Because of Jesus' death, Satan's accusations against Christians are powerless and our eternal future is assured.

---

11. **How is Esther different in verses 15-17 from the Esther of verse 11? What do you think has changed her?**
The truth, expressed in Mordecai's loving and faith-filled challenge, is what sparks the change in Esther. Initially timid and terrified (v 11-12), Esther decides to take up Mordecai's challenge with determination and resolve. Her comment: "If I perish, I perish" sounds fatalistic rather than fully trusting in God at this point. Yet she calls the people to fast as she chooses to risk her life, suggesting that her fear of God is growing greater than her fear of man.

12. How should we respond in a situation where we are fearful of doing what God wants? What will help us overcome our fear?

It's faith that changes our fear to courage, and it's God's word that equips us for every good work. So we need to read, listen to and learn from God's word, with the aim of building up our faith in God. Why not discuss how we can help one another practically to build up faith in God from his word?

5

The Pride Before the Fall

Esther 4:15 - 5:14

The Big Idea

Humble reliance on God, seen in making prayer a priority, results in wisdom, courage and hope, leading to behaviour that glorifies him.

Summary

Esther calls the Jews to fast for three days in preparation for her appearance before the king. On that day, as she approaches the throne, he welcomes her. He recognises that she has a request to make but, instead of making it, she invites him, along with Haman, to one banquet and then, intriguingly, to another the following day at which the mystery will be revealed! Haman is ecstatic at the recognition he has received... until he sees his enemy, Mordecai, still refusing to bow to him. This starts him on a rollercoaster of emotions, which ends in delight as he has pole/gallows erected from which to impale/hang Mordecai.

There is a striking contrast in this part of the story between Haman's emotional instability, which flows from his conceit and pride, and Esther's calm purpose—the fruit of her humble dependence on God for the outcome of her mission. This humility towards God is seen in the way she commits herself and her people to an extended time of prayer and fasting before taking action.

NOTE: It's important for your group to understand that although prayer is not explicitly mentioned here, fasting in Jewish culture would certainly include prayer. (See references to Daniel and Joel in question 2.)

The challenges of this session are for us to show the same commitment to reliance on God in prayer, and to live lives of true humility. Today this is seen first and foremost in seeking God's mercy, shown to us in the saving death and resurrection of Jesus Christ.

Optional Extra

A "Guess who in three clues" game, or anagrams, using characters from the Bible who demonstrate the truth that God raises up the humble and brings down the proud. (This only works for groups whose members have a good amount of Bible knowledge.) Use these examples:

The humble: Abram (Genesis 13); Moses (Numbers 12); Ruth; David (1 Samuel 24); Abigail (1 Samuel 25); Solomon (1 Kings 3); Josiah (2 Kings 22); Mary (Luke 1); the sinful woman (Luke 7); the sick woman (Luke 8); Lazarus (Luke 16), etc.

The proud: Goliath (1 Samuel 17); Rehoboam (1 Kings 12); Uzziah (2 Chronicles 26); Nebuchadnezzar (Daniel 4); the rich man (Luke 16); Herod (Acts 12), etc.

An alternative option is to find and print up some quotations on the subject of humility (e.g. www.quotegarden.com/humility.html). Use these as a basis for discussion e.g. Do people agree/disagree? What truth about pride and humility does each quotation highlight?

Guidance for Questions

1. **Describe a time when you felt supported by the prayers and love of others.**

   Talk about what this felt like and how those prayers were answered. This question prepares the way for the main theme of this session, which is the importance of humble reliance on God in prayer.

2. **What does Esther call the Jews in Susa to do? Why? (Read Daniel 9:3 and Joel 2:12-13.)**

   Esther calls for three days of corporate fasting before she approaches King Xerxes. She demonstrates personal (and calls for national) reliance on God for wisdom, courage and success. Like Daniel before her (who was among one of the first exiles when Babylon conquered Jerusalem), she recognises that without God's intervention and help there is little hope for her or her people. She is responding to God's clear commands with trust in his promises of deliverance, like that found in Joel 2:12-13. Prayer and repentance (as mentioned in Daniel and Joel) would be expected to accompany fasting—the purpose of fasting being to draw the attention away from self and towards God.

- ***OPTIONAL: Look back to 4:3. Why do you think she calls the Jews to do something they were already doing?***

  Perhaps Esther wasn't aware of the fasting going on already (she hadn't known of Haman's plot until now). Also the Jews had fasted spontaneously but Esther now requests it for her specific task.

3. **If you had been one of the Jews asked by Esther to fast, what do you think you would have prayed for?**

   Answers could include: guidance, wisdom and courage for Esther; a warm welcome from the king; a good opportunity for her to speak; for

Esther's words to be well received; judgment on Haman; justice and deliverance for the Jews; God's name to be honoured among the Gentiles.

4. **Read 2 Thessalonians 1:11-12. How and what do Paul, Silas and Timothy pray for their fellow Christians?**
Paul, Timothy and Silas pray for the believers in Thessalonica ("we constantly pray for you") because they want them to be faithful by glorifying God through doing his will. This happens when the Thessalonians behave in keeping with their identity as Christians ("worthy of his calling"), and display good works that flow out of their faith in God's power ("your every deed prompted by faith"), so bringing glory to Christ.

- **In 2 Thessalonians 3:1-2, what things do they ask their fellow Christians to pray for them?**
That the gospel will spread rapidly and be honoured, and that they would be delivered from opponents of the gospel who would persecute them.

5. **In what ways is this an encouraging start to Esther's mission?**
She gains smooth and easy access to Xerxes, who greets her with so much pleasure that he is eager to grant her any request. Both he and Haman are free to drop everything to attend her banquet, which is such a success that they are both eager to repeat the experience the following day—again their schedules are free. Esther is calm enough to host her meal while holding both her nerve and her tongue. Haman suspects nothing but instead leaves the first banquet with even more of an over-inflated view of himself, triggering a chain of events that will lead to his own personal disaster.

6. **Why do you think she delays making her true request on both occasions?**
We will see that Esther has a carefully planned strategy, which is completely in step with God's timing. It seems that God gave her the guidance and wisdom she needed during her period of fasting. Her understanding of court etiquette and the king has also helped her to evaluate the risks of blurting out her request immediately, and to take the best alternative course of action. She would be aware of the (blind) faith Xerxes has in Haman, and the dangers of accusing Haman straight away. And since she has not been in the king's presence for over 30 days (4:11), she needs first to spend time reminding her husband of her worth and showing that she can be trusted.

7. **What qualities do you think Esther shows here?**
The peace with which she acts and speaks indicates a heart completely at rest in God. She is self-controlled, patient, discreet, wise and humble. She also uses the resources at her disposal, including her ability to offer royal hospitality fit for a king and a prime minister. No doubt she makes the most of her beauty in terms of

both her appearance and her character. No doubt too that the food and wine were delicious.

8. **Track Haman's changing emotions and the reasons for each one.**
See below for Haman's emotional journey through these verses. (If it's helpful, copy this diagram onto a whiteboard / flip chart.)
Haman's changing emotions are closely linked with his massive ego and his obsession with power and approval. He is influenced by how he thinks others view him. So when honoured by Esther and Xerxes, he is elated; yet he quickly becomes furious because Mordecai still refuses to bow to him. Haman restrains himself by returning to his flattering wife and by throwing a bragging party. This lifts his spirits, which reach the heights again as he recalls how he has been uniquely recognised by Esther, and as he contemplates the next day's feast. Down he plummets again, however, when he remembers Mordecai, yet regains his spirits as he plots his revenge.

9. **What explains the difference between Haman's emotional instability and Esther's patience and self-control, do you think? (You might like to read Galatians 5:16-22.)**
Haman's hatred, rage and selfish ambition are the fruit of his sinful nature, by which he is deceived and enslaved (Galatians 5:16-21; Titus 3:3). He is the centre of his universe, and his emotions reflect whether or not others treat him as he feels he deserves to be treated. Esther, by contrast, because she depends on God and puts her hope in him, is freed to be patient and self-controlled in difficult circumstances (Galatians 5:22). This is an example of the quiet and gentle spirit mentioned by Peter in 1 Peter 3:4-5 (session 2, question 4).

10. **How do we change from being like Haman (an emotional rollercoaster) to being more like Esther in her patience and self-control? What guidance do these passages give us?**
- **Galatians 5:19-26**
First, we must "belong to Christ Jesus" (v 24), and "live by the Spirit" (v 25)—i.e. those who trust in Christ to be rescued from sin receive from God his new life within us. It's important that we understand that we cannot simply "turn over a new leaf".

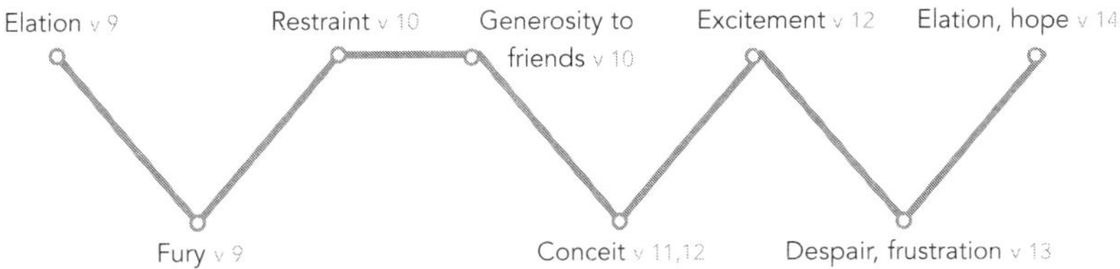

Secondly, those who belong to Christ have "crucified the flesh (sinful nature)" (v 24)—we have said goodbye to the old way of life and we resist its power over us. Those who live by the Spirit "keep in step with the Spirit"—i.e. live in a new way that pleases God. Make sure people see the combination of God's work in us—giving us new life in Christ, and our responsibility—to live out the new life we have been given.

- **James 4:7-10**
  If we humble ourselves before the Lord, he will lift us up. As God's people we do not need to concern ourselves with our own status, honour, security or image in this world. Our focus should be on a right relationship with God—submission, responsiveness, receiving forgiveness, confessing our sins and humility (v 7-10). God will do everything else that is required and we can patiently and quietly trust in his sovereignty and perfect plans.

Explore More

- ***Read Proverbs 11:2; 29:23; 16:18. What warnings are we given about pride?***
  It is dangerous, even deadly. It leads to disgrace, humiliation and destruction.

- ***Why do you think God hates sinful pride?***
  It means we are not giving God the glory he deserves. We're relying on our own understanding, strength and abilities rather than on God, who has given us all we have. Pride comes from lack of submission to our Creator and is based on the lie that we don't need him. It is therefore a form of idolatry that leads to every other kind of sin.

- ***What does Jesus say about humility? Read Matthew 18:1-4 and Luke 18:9-14.***
  - *Matthew 18:1-4: Jesus is answering the disciples' foolish question about who will be greatest in God's kingdom (v 1). Without humility we can't enter the kingdom of heaven—we can't be saved from our sins and become one of God's people. Jesus made the point about becoming like a little child not to teach that we must be innocent (children are sinners too) but to illustrate humility. Children back then were considered of least importance. And all children are characterised by ready dependence on those who care for them—so we should recognise our humble dependence on God, our heavenly Father.*
  - *Luke 18:9-14: Jesus shows what the humility that qualifies us for God's kingdom looks like. It means admitting our sinfulness, refusing to justify ourselves and instead throwing ourselves on God's mercy.*

- ***How did Jesus show humility? Read 1 Peter 2:21-24.***
  Jesus was able to humbly endure the suffering of the cross, and so achieve

salvation and healing for his people, because he entrusted himself to his perfectly just Father (v 23). Christians are called to do the same (v 21).

- ***What does humility look like today?*** *Humility in the Bible is not about our personality but about our attitude to God and our relationship with him, shaped by the gospel. Those who are truly humble today are those who call for, receive and live in reliance on God's mercy towards sinners in Jesus Christ (like the tax collector in Luke 18:9-14). In other words, you cannot be truly humble if you are not a Christian.*

6

A Rollercoaster Ride

Esther 6 - 7

The Big Idea

God's timing is perfect: he will judge his enemies and vindicate his people at precisely the right time.

Summary

The king discovers that Mordecai has been overlooked for saving his life, and he determines to set things right. When Haman walks in, full of his plans to impale/hang Mordecai, Xerxes asks him how he should honour the man of his choosing. Conceited Haman thinks the king must be speaking of him. Xerxes is delighted with Haman's suggestions, but Haman is humiliated when he discovers Mordecai is the one to be honoured, while he is the one to lead and announce Mordecai. Haman's friends recognise that both he and his plans are now doomed.

Immediately afterwards, Haman is rushed to Esther's second banquet, where she gives a bold and impassioned speech, naming Haman as the instigator of evil plans to destroy her and her people. Xerxes storms outside in anger. He returns to find a terrified and desperate Haman falling across Esther's couch. Thinking that the queen is being accosted, he commands that Haman be executed on the pole/gallows prepared for Mordecai.

This session shows that God knows and controls every detail of our lives. Although humans have many plans, God's plans are the ones that will triumph. God is sovereign over both the godly and the ungodly, over rulers and ordinary people like us. All things are at his disposal—time, sleep, books, banquets, seemingly insignificant events and even a set of gallows! He delights in answering his people's prayers often in the most unexpected ways. His timing is perfect—he is to be trusted at all times.

Optional Extra

1. (Relates to theme of God's perfect timing) Play a game that depends on the right timing e.g. numerous computer/console games; swingball; mini ball maze, etc.
2. (Relates to 6:1) How much sleep do you need? Discuss the reasons why it can be difficult to sleep. Share funny stories about sleep: sleep walking, talking, snoring, etc. What can help with sleeplessness?

Guidance for Questions

1. **Have you ever faced something difficult, and then discovered (perhaps much later) that God was clearly working everything out behind the scenes? What was it?**

   This question introduces the idea that God sovereignly intervenes in ways we do not expect and are often not aware of. It's good, therefore, to look back over incidents in life where, with hindsight, we can clearly see that he has been working things out for our good.

2. **How does a forgotten event (recorded back in 2:21-23) suddenly become hugely significant (v 1-3)?**

   The king can't sleep and so asks for the records of his reign to be read to him. He discovers that Mordecai was never rewarded for saving his life and he determines to set the matter straight.

3. **How might you have felt if, like Mordecai, your act of loyalty to the king had been ignored? Or if you knew that a gallows had been prepared for you by a powerful enemy?**

   We might feel disappointed and discouraged, perhaps even resentful at this lack of recognition; and the apparent success of powerful enemies will probably make us anxious. But this all changes when we can trust that God is sovereignly, though invisibly, at work. This question will help your group to put themselves in Mordecai's shoes, in preparation for the following application question, which deals with the shift in our perspective on disappointment or anxiety when we trust in God's sovereignty.

4. **Read Psalm 31:15; Acts 1:7. What can we learn from the timing of the king's discovery of Mordecai's loyalty?**

   The timing of these events is beyond the likelihood of coincidence. If they had occurred even one night later, then Mordecai would have died and the rescue of the Jewish nation would have been in jeopardy. From this we learn that God knows and controls every detail of our lives; his timing is perfect and his purposes will be achieved; he is both sovereign and faithful; and therefore he is to be trusted at all times.

   Psalm 31:15 reminds us that our times are in God's hands and we can trust him for the future and cry to him with confidence for deliverance. In Acts 1:7, just before Jesus ascends into heaven, he tells his disciples that although we don't know the future, God the Father has set dates by his own authority. This points us to our ultimate deliverance as believers when Jesus will return in the same way that he went (Acts 1:11).

- **What does this remind us about kings and rulers? (See Proverbs 21:1.)**
  Proverbs 21:1 states that the hearts of kings and rulers are in God's control. This fact is clearly illustrated in Xerxes' inability to sleep, his choice of reading material, the recognition of his oversight of Mordecai, his remorse and his determination to put things right immediately. As God's people, this means that we need have no anxiety about the opposition or failings of others, even of those who seem to have great power over our lives.

Explore More

- ***Read Romans 5:6. How was this true in the past?***
  The apostle Paul asserts that the timing of Christ's death on the cross was perfectly set by God.
- ***Read 1 Corinthians 4:5. How will this be true in the future?***
  The timing of Christ's return to judge the world and to vindicate his people has also been perfectly set by God.
- ***Read 2 Peter 3:3-12. Where do non-believers go wrong (v 3-7)?***
  Because God has held back his judgment until now, they imagine things will continue as they always have (v 4) and so judgment will never come. They choose to forget that God has already shown himself both prepared and able to judge the world, at the time of the flood (v 6).
- ***What must we understand, to avoid falling into the same unbelief?***
- ***v 8***
  God's view of the passage of time is very different from ours. What seems a never-ending age to us is momentary in God's eyes and vice versa.
- ***v 9***
  The apparent delay in coming judgment is not because God is failing to keep his promise but because in his mercy he gives time for as many people as possible to repent and trust in Christ for salvation.
- ***v 10***
  It is an unchangeable fact that God's day of judgment will come.
- ***When we trust in God's perfect timing, what difference does it make in our lives (v 11-12)?***
  Our lives will be affected by our belief in the certainty of God's future judgment. We become holy and godly, and full of hope and joy.

5. **Reread Esther 6:6-9. What do these verses show us about Haman?**

   After the honour given him by the queen, and filled with anticipation at the death of Mordecai (the one blot on his landscape), Haman is even more puffed up with pride and conceit than before. The over-inflated view he has of himself is revealed in 6:6: "Haman thought to himself, 'Who is there that the king would rather honour than me?'" He is almost drooling as he describes a reward that he feels would fit him well. Up until now Haman has been portrayed as chilling and dangerous. However these and the following verses mark him out not only as foolish but also as ridiculous. One far greater than Haman is at work and he doesn't stand a chance.

6. **What do his advisers and wife recognise in verse 13? How does this differ from 5:14?**

   After the events of the previous few hours, Haman's wife and advisers recognise for the first time that because Mordecai is a Jew (one of God's chosen people), Haman doesn't stand a chance against him. It's regrettable for Haman that they didn't recognise this before they encouraged him in his vendetta against Mordecai and his people (5:14).

- **As Haman is rushed off to Esther's second banquet, how do you think his expectations and feelings might have changed since the first one?**

  At this point Haman still doesn't know who Esther is. He probably doesn't think the day could get much worse. We can assume however that his expectations and joy in the occasion are not as great as they were the day before. It seems that there has been no opportunity to refresh himself emotionally or physically after the trauma and busyness of the day, and he must feel unprepared for such a special event.

7. **Describe Esther's speech in verses 3-4.**

   - *Respectful:* "If I have found favour with you, Your Majesty, and if it pleases you, grant me..." "I would have kept quiet, because no such distress would justify disturbing the king."
   - *Direct:* "Grant me my life—this is my petition. And spare my people—this is my request. For I and my people have been sold to be destroyed, killed and annihilated."
   - *Courageous:* She identifies herself with her people, knowing that the king has (however unknowingly) signed their death warrant.
   - *Passionate:* Her choice of graphic language shows great strength of feeling.
   - *Restrained:* She still at this point does not name Haman as the instigator of this plot.
   - *Dignified:* She is still reclining on her couch, it seems, right up until the end of the chapter.

An alternative way of answering this question would be to write up the words listed above and ask your group to identify how Esther's speech fits these descriptions.

- **From verse 5, why do you think Esther can now be confident that Xerxes is on her side?**
Esther's plan and speech have effectively reeled Xerxes in. Xerxes asks her directly who would dare do this and where he is. Perhaps with the added confidence that the recognition of Mordecai has brought, she names Haman, boldly describing him as vile, and labelling him "an adversary and enemy".

8. **How does Xerxes react? Why do you think he goes out into the palace garden?**
Xerxes reacts with shock and rage. He is so agitated that not only does he go into the palace garden, but he leaves his wine behind! You could use the questions below to keep your group focused on the theme of God's sovereignty.

   We are not told why he goes out into the garden. It's possible however that he needs space to grasp the implications of Esther's revelation—that the man in whom he has unhesitatingly invested his own authority has actually used him to bring about the destruction of his own wife and all her people. The ruler of the world's greatest empire has been kept in the dark, betrayed by his right-hand man, and tricked into authorising a genocide that he has never even dreamed of.

- ***OPTIONAL: What do the words "in a rage" (v 7) tell us about the king's state of mind?***
His anger is out of control. The implications for Haman are truly perilous—he cannot hope that the king will temper his anger with reason, righteousness or compassion, nor can he predict how far the king will take his anger.

- ***OPTIONAL: Why can Esther remain confident of the right outcome?***
Even though the king's rage is uncontrolled and unpredictable, Esther can trust that the king's heart is in the hand of the Lord (Proverbs 21:1). The king's uncontrolled anger is under God's control, and will be used for his purposes.

9. **How does Haman respond (v 6-8), and how is his fate sealed (v 8-10)?**
He is shocked and terrified. Even if he'd realised that he wouldn't succeed against Mordecai, he had no idea that his own death blow would come through Esther, who he didn't know was a Jewess or related to Mordecai. He takes the opportunity of the king's absence to appeal to Esther. Dignity gone, he throws himself onto her couch as he begs for mercy. So extreme is his behaviour that when Xerxes returns, he mistakenly thinks Esther is being accosted. This is enough for the king to condemn him to death immediately, and at Harbona's suggestion, Haman is hanged on the gallows meant for Mordecai. The devious

Haman has been out-played and out-manoeuvred.

10. **How can these chapters help our faith in God to grow? (Proverbs 19:21 might help you.)**
Proverbs 19:21 tells us that although humans have many plans, God's plans are the ones that will triumph. Esther 6 and 7 are a great example of that fact. God is sovereign over both the godly and the ungodly, over rulers and ordinary people like us. He judges the proud and exalts the humble. All things are at his disposal—time, sleep, books, banquets, seemingly insignificant events and even a set of gallows! He delights in answering his people's prayers often in the most unexpected ways. He is to be trusted at all times. And although these events were deadly serious at the time, we who have the privilege of reading this account can appreciate the humour with which it is written, along with the various dramatic twists and turns. Surely God wants us to enjoy and marvel at his ingenuity!

11. **Read Matthew 10:17-20, 28. How are the lessons of this session reinforced by Jesus' teaching to his disciples about persecution?**
Jesus warns his disciples of the extreme kind of persecution that they will experience for his sake. He commands them not to worry, assuring them that the Holy Spirit will give them the words to speak. In fact, they will be aware that God himself is speaking through them. In verse 28 he reminds them that it is foolish to fear humans more than God. Humans have limited power over our earthly bodies, while God has eternal power over our souls as well as our bodies.

- **How can these lessons help us when we face opposition for following Jesus Christ?**
If people are willing, ask them to share situations in which they faced, or are facing, opposition for their Christian faith. Discuss how the lessons of this session can encourage and strengthen them in these situations. It may be helpful to have an example of your own to start with.

7

A Great Deliverance

Esther 8 - 10

The Big Idea

With God's help his people triumph over their enemies and so celebration and remembering God's deliverance becomes part of living as God's people.

Summary

Mordecai is promoted to Haman's position. Despite Esther's achievements however, the lives of her people remain in peril. Again, she comes before the king to plead tearfully for them. Xerxes gives full resources and authority for Esther and Mordecai to send a message to all Jews, giving them the right to protect themselves and retaliate against their enemies.

On the day that the enemies of the Jews hope to annihilate them, the Jews overpower their enemies instead. More than 75,000 die, including the ten sons of Haman. Afterwards the Jews celebrate, and an annual festival is established to commemorate God's great deliverance of his people.

This points ahead to God's deliverance of sinners from all nations through Christ. There are striking parallels between the two rescues: God's deliverance is celebrated before the final battle takes place; the Jews' celebrations are sparked by the sight of their leader exalted by the king; though they have received the good news of the king's intervention on their behalf against their enemies, they are still called on to go and fight the enemy; with final victory comes rest. Application focuses on commemorating and celebrating God's deliverance through Christ, while also being prepared to "fight the good fight of faith".

Optional Extra

Two ideas...

1. Share testimonies of how God saved you. Try to relate people's stories to that of God's deliverance of Esther and her people, and the truths about God highlighted in these studies.
2. If you are feeling more ambitious, arrange an extra review session. Give your group (perhaps divided into smaller groups) time to look through Esther and pinpoint the main message—the theme of God sovereignly working even in the darkest of times for the good of his people and the glory of his name. Esther is fundamentally about God the Deliverer. His rescue comes in part through Esther and Mordecai, who both point to Jesus Christ, the greater Deliverer, coming nearly 500 years later to save his people from their sins. After briefly reviewing Esther, group members (individually or in groups) can create a presentation for people who know nothing about this true

story. This could be done as a drama, news report, song, rap or poem, quiz, etc. Encourage creativity with the presentation, but the content should be based on the main points learned from Esther. As well as being fun, this sort of review helps people realise how much they have learned, and the value of passing that on to others.

Guidance for Questions

1. **Describe a time in your life when you thought you had completed a challenge but then found another one ahead. How did it feel?**
   This sets the scene for this session.

2. **How are Esther and Mordecai honoured after the king's fury has subsided (v 1-2)?**
   Esther is given Haman's estate (v 1) and Mordecai the royal signet ring taken from Haman prior to his execution (v 2). The honour and authority that Haman enjoyed is now Mordecai's. Esther gives Haman's estate to Mordecai to manage.

- **Why is this an encouraging sign?**
  Esther again has an opportunity to speak out. This outcome was unimaginable just hours before, when Haman was the king's favourite and Mordecai hated by Haman. The king now trusts with royal authority Mordecai, who he had probably never even noticed before. God has completely reversed the fortunes of Mordecai and Esther, so they can have even greater confidence that the king will now act for the deliverance of their people.

3. **Why is it still difficult (and even dangerous) for Esther to make a second request of the king, do you think? (See 4:11.)**
   Because Xerxes has been so good to her already—believing her, executing Haman and honouring both her and Mordecai, she could be seen as ungrateful and nagging, putting her people before her husband, and questioning his goodness and wisdom (since he had sanctioned the Jewish genocide, however unwittingly). Again she has to come uninvited before the king (though he again extends his sceptre in mercy, v 4). And she comes weeping (something highly dangerous, as we saw in session 4).

- **What do you think motivates her and gives her courage?**
  Even though her safety and honour, and Mordecai's, are secured, great love for her people motivates her to sacrifice all that for their safety. Surely the amazing way in which she has seen God work in the last few days has built her courage and dispelled her fear.

4. **How is the situation dealt with (v 9-14)? What shows how God has completely turned the situation around?**
   The situation is resolved immediately, thoroughly, and fairly. The system Haman used for evil, Mordecai now uses for good.

- **v 9—compare 3:12**
  He employs the same royal secretaries and the same legal system.
- **v 10—compare 3:10, 12b**
  He uses the same authority (the king's name and signet ring).
- **v 11-14—compare 3:13-15**
  The same messengers and horses are sent out with the new edict. Xerxes shows absolute trust in Esther and Mordecai, just as he once trusted Haman (3:10-11). He tells them to do whatever is needed to pass another law in his name. He puts at their disposal every authority and resource available. And the new edict is fair: the Jews are to destroy only armed forces in self defence, rather than attacking the whole population. (Compare 8:11 with 3:13.)

5. **What do you notice about the celebrations in verses 15-17?**
   Mordecai emerges from the royal palace, splendid in royal robes, leading to spontaneous and wholehearted celebrations, first in Susa and then throughout the empire. As the decree reaches each province and city, a public festival and holiday is declared.

- ***OPTIONAL: The following questions draw out some important aspects, which are helpful for answering question 7.***
- ***What sparks these celebrations?***
  The public appearance of Mordecai, resplendently dressed and displaying honour and authority given to him by the king, and now clearly recognised as the leader of his people.
- ***At what point do the celebrations take place? Why is that significant?***
  The celebrations take place before the day when the Jews will fight against their enemies. In other words, the final battle has not yet been won. The Jewish people are already confident of final victory.

6. **What is the impact of these events on people of other nationalities? (Compare verse 17 with Isaiah 65:1.)**
   They fear the Jews—in fact, many convert to Judaism. These people don't seem to have been seeking God previously, yet God has shown himself and his power through these events in Persia. This is what was prophesied in Isaiah 65:1.

7. **Read Luke 19:10; Romans 6:23; Acts 2:21. What is the great deliverance all Christians have experienced?**
   As Luke 19:10 and Romans 6:23 explain, Jesus came to look for those who are "lost", who need to be delivered from sin and death. The testimony of all Christians is that when we called to God for rescue, he rescued us (Acts 2:21). This is a good opportunity for you to check that your group understand the good news of Jesus Christ. If necessary, take them through a brief explanation of how Jesus rescues us from sin and death (e.g. 2 Timothy 1:9-10 or Titus 3:3-7 and 2:11-14).

- **What other parallels can you see between this part of the story of Esther and the gospel?**
    - *Celebration now:* Joy, seen in singing and thanksgiving, is a major part of the Christian life (Colossians 3:15-17).
    - *Our King glorified:* Although the world does not recognise Jesus, Christians see him "now crowned with glory and honour" (Hebrews 2:9), and our living relationship with him gives us joy even in difficult circumstances.
    - *Victory certain but not yet completed:* Christians are confident of Christ's final victory, even as we continue to battle against God's enemy and his schemes (Ephesians 6:11-13).
    - *Effect on other nations:* God shows himself to people of all nations through what he has done for his people i.e. when Christians tell others the gospel of Jesus Christ and how he has saved them (Luke 24:47; Acts 8:1, 4).

8. **For what reasons can Christians sometimes fail to respond to God's deliverance with joy, gladness and celebration?**
   Our response should be great and overflowing joy that is obvious to others. We lose our joy because we have lost sight of what Christ did for us on the cross.

   The root cause is failing to believe the truth of the gospel—why we need Christ to save us, all that he has done for us, and why only he can rescue us. Possibly we don't really believe that there will be a final judgment or that we deserve judgment. This lack of belief in God's truth means...
    - when we're tempted, we drift into idolatry, treasuring other things more than Christ.
    - when we sin, guilt weighs us down and steals our joy.
    - when suffering comes, we have no confidence in the Christian hope.
    - we become self-righteous, so we don't value Christ, we look down on others, and we end up proud and self-congratulatory instead of thankful and joyful in the Lord.

- ***OPTIONAL: What's the remedy for lack of joy and thankfulness in a Christian?***
  We need to go back to God's word and learn again the good news of Jesus Christ—to read or listen to it, hear it taught and preached, study it, think about it and how it affects our everyday lives, pray about it, live it out, talk about it with Christian brothers and sisters, and share it with others.

- **What impact can we have on others when they witness the effects of this good news in our lives?**
  Genuine joy will have a great impact on those around us. This supernatural joy is especially powerful when people see it in times of sadness and hardship.

9. From verses 1-17, what things happened to make this possible?

- The Jews were ready on the day previously set by Haman (v 2).
- They were united, gathering together in their cities (v 2).
- They were feared. People were so intimidated that they couldn't stand up to them (v 2).
- They were empowered by Mordecai's prominent and increasing authority (v 3-4) and by Esther's courage and determination (v 12-13).
- They were helped by the empire's officials (v 3) and by Xerxes himself, who approved both a second day of fighting in Susa and the hanging of Haman's sons (v 14).
- The Jews fought valiantly and honourably until their task was completed (v 5-10, 14-16).

- ***OPTIONAL: How did the Jews show thoroughness in the battle against their enemies (v 5-10, 13-16)?***
  Altogether, 810 enemies were killed in Susa (including the ten sons of Haman, all named, whose bodies were also publicly disgraced by hanging) and 75,000 throughout the rest of the empire.

- ***How did they show restraint (v 10, 15, 16—compare 3:13)?***
  Haman had called for the annihilation of all Jews (including women and children) and for their possessions to be plundered. The Jews however, as permitted, only killed armed men who were enemies (8:11; 9:6, 15). They fought only in self-defence (v 16). And they did not take plunder (mentioned three times), even though the edict permitted this. (See end of 8:11.)

Explore More

- ***Read 2 Corinthians 10:3-5. The apostle Paul is telling us about the fight that followers of Jesus are to be engaged in. What does he say about...***
- ***the battle?***
  Although we are real humans living in a physical world, this battle is of a spiritual nature.
- ***the enemy?***
  Our enemy is seen in the satanic and human arguments, lies, beliefs, thoughts and ideas that people use to keep out the truth of the gospel.
- ***the weapons? (See also Ephesians 6:17.)***
  This battle will not be won with physical strength or strategies. God gives us the weapons that will be powerful and effective against our spiritual enemy (e.g. the sword of the Spirit, which is God's word, Ephesians 6:17).
- ***the aim?***
  To rescue people from Satan by spreading knowledge of and obedience to Christ.

---

10. In 1 Timothy 6:12 the apostle Paul tells us to "fight the good fight of

the faith". What is involved in doing this, do you think?

Paul urges Timothy to be a brave soldier and "fight the good fight of the faith". The Greek for "fight" gives us the word "agonise" and describes concentration, discipline and extreme effort. The word "good" indicates that it is a cause worth fighting for! Confidence in the reality of eternal life gives us the right perspective and motivation needed to keep going in the battle, just as the Jews' confidence in future deliverance strengthened them against their enemies (Esther 8:17; 9:1).

- **Read 2 Timothy 2:1-6, and then complete the following in your own words: A good soldier...**
  - is strong in Christ's grace.
  - understands the priority of true teaching and passes it on.
  - endures hardship.
  - is not distracted.
  - wants to please the one who has enlisted them (Christ).
  - follows the Lord's commands.
  - works hard.
  - looks forward to their reward.

  Discuss what these qualities will look like in your daily lives.

11. **How did the Jews respond to victory (9:17-19)?**

    With rest, celebration, feasting, joy and the giving of presents.

    NOTE: The fact that the Jews "rested" is significant. Throughout the Bible "rest" is God's promise and goal for his people, and is often mentioned when circumstances reach an "ideal" state, e.g. when God finished the work of creation (Genesis 2:2); when Israel completed the invasion of the promised land (Joshua 21:44); King David at the height of his reign (2 Samuel 7:1); King Solomon at the consecration of the temple (1 Kings 8:56). These are all pictures of the ultimate rest found through Christ (Matthew 11:29) in the new heaven and earth (Hebrews 4:8-11).

    - **Why did Mordecai (v 20-22) and Esther (v 29) act as they did?**

      Mordecai recorded everything that had happened and set up an annual celebration because something truly remarkable had occurred that he didn't want to be forgotten. Purim was established so that the Jews would remember God's deliverance in a way that would encourage them and bring them hope for future trials. Mordecai wanted God to be glorified not only among his generation, but for generations to come. Esther wrote a second letter because she too saw the importance of these plans.

12. **Share some practical things that we can do to help each other in this (individually, in families and as churches).**

    Some suggestions to get the discussion going:

    - Regular times of prayer and Bible-reading or listening (individually and as families)

- Meeting regularly with God's people
- Serving Christ's body—the church
- Listening to Christian music
- Reading books that will encourage us and build us up in faith
- Sharing Communion / the Lord's Supper
- Getting involved at some level in sharing the gospel with others;
- Conferences, inspirational Christian gatherings, singing, etc.

Explore the Whole Range

Old Testament, including:

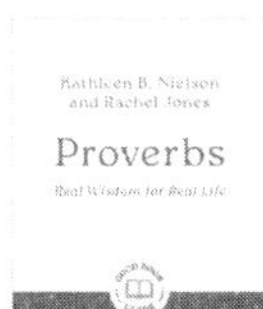

New Testament, including:

Topical, including:

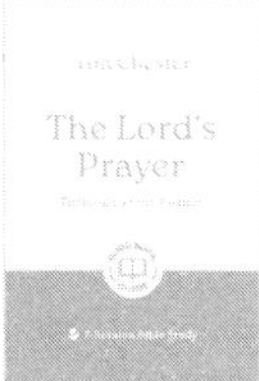

Flexible and easy to use, with over 50 titles available, Good Book Guides are perfect for both groups and individuals.

thegoodbook.com/gbgs
thegoodbook.co.uk/gbgs
thegoodbook.com.au/gbgs

God's Word For You

Accessible Commentaries That Everyone Can Enjoy

Old Testament, including:

New Testament, including:

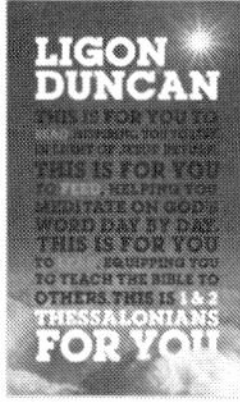

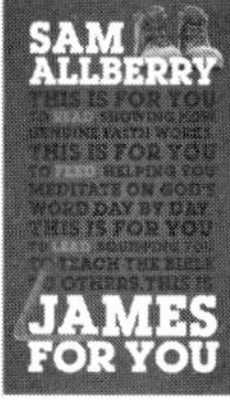

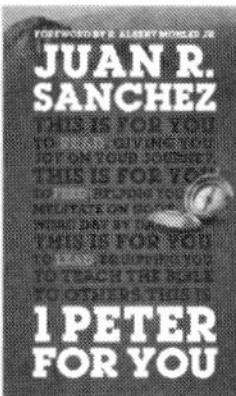

Less academic than a traditional commentary, these expository guides take you verse by verse through books of the Bible in an accessible, applied way. These flexible resources can enrich your personal devotions, help you lead small-group studies, or aid your sermon preparations.

Use with accompanying Good Book Guides to study these books of the Bible in small groups.

thegoodbook.com/for-you
thegoodbook.co.uk/for-you
thegoodbook.com.au/for-you

BIBLICAL | RELEVANT | ACCESSIBLE

At The Good Book Company we are dedicated to helping Christians and local churches grow. We believe that God's growth process always starts with hearing clearly what he has said to us through his timeless and flawless word—the Bible.

Ever since we opened our doors in 1991, we have been striving to produce resources that are biblical, relevant, and accessible. By God's grace, we have grown to become an international publisher, encouraging ordinary Christians of every age and stage and every background and denomination to live for Christ day by day and equipping churches to grow in their knowledge of God, their love for one another, and the effectiveness of their outreach.

Call one of our friendly team for a discussion of your needs or visit one of our local websites for more information on the resources and services we provide.

Your friends at The Good Book Company

thegoodbook.com | thegoodbook.co.uk
thegoodbook.com.au | thegoodbook.co.nz